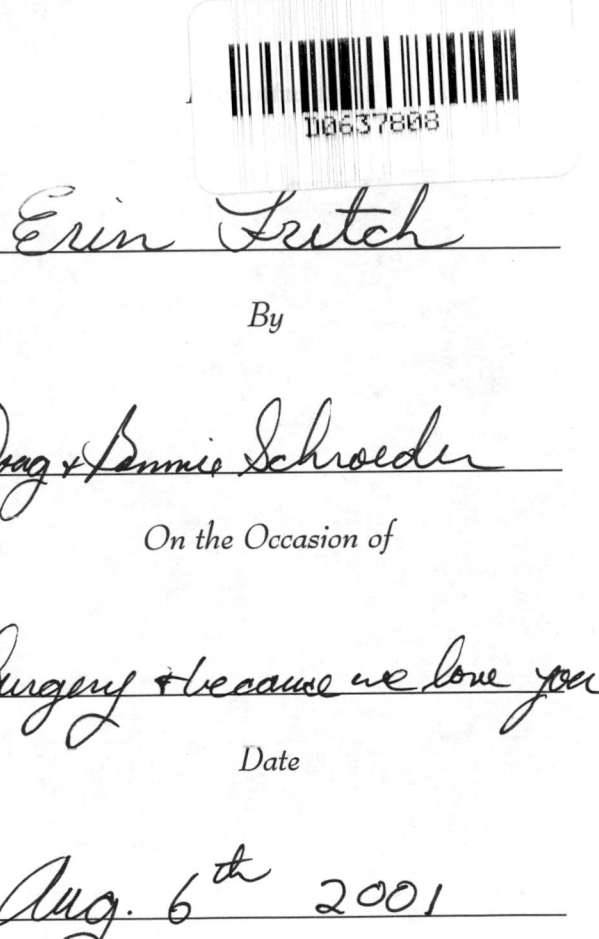

10637808

_Erin Fritch_

By

_Doug & Bonnie Schroeder_

On the Occasion of

_Surgery & because we love you_

Date

_Aug. 6th 2001_

# A HEART LIKE HIS

## DISCOVERING THE HEART OF JESUS IN THE FRUIT OF THE SPIRIT

Mike & Amy Nappa

BARBOUR
PUBLISHING, INC.
Uhrichsville, Ohio

# A HEART
# LIKE HIS

Published by Barbour Publishing, Inc., P.O. Box 719, Uhrichsville, OH 44683 http://www.barbourbooks.com

Member of the
Evangelical Christian
Publishers Association

Printed in the United States of America.

*This book is lovingly dedicated to the memory of Wilfred Townsend, a man who exhibited a heart like Christ's in our every encounter with him.*

*Though he passed away more than two years ago, we are thankful for Grand Wil's example and still remember him with great fondness, anticipating the day when we will be joyfully reunited with him in heaven.*

# CONTENTS

*Against such things there is no law!*

# INTRODUCTION:
## PAUL'S LITTLE GROCERY LIST

He rattles them off quickly, as if he's simply listing the first things that come to his mind. "The fruit of the Spirit," Paul says in the book of Galatians, "is love, joy, peace, patience, kindness, goodness, faithfulness, gentleness and self-control" (5:22–23 NIV).

Then, almost as an afterthought, he adds, "Against such things there is no law."

I read those words today and wonder: Did Paul realize he was writing a letter that would someday be called the Word of God? Did he know the difference his little grocery list of character qualities would make in the lives of millions of people? In the lives of people like me and you?

Honestly, I don't know. But I do know the words Paul spoke in Galatians 5:22–23 carry with them a challenge—and an invitation. A challenge to become the kind of person whose life is characterized by these qualities; an invitation to allow God's Spirit to work in our hearts and make the fulfillment of that challenge possible.

Which brings us to this book. Not long ago,

my wife, Amy, and I sat down and began asking ourselves, "What does the fruit of the Spirit really mean? How does it bring about in us a heart like Christ's?" This book is the result of our searching thus far. Of course it doesn't contain all the answers, but we hope it has a few. Of course it doesn't ask all the questions either, but we hope it inspires a few new ones.

So are you ready to join us in our exploration of Paul's little grocery list? Then turn the page and let's get on our way. Our prayer is that reading this book will bless you as much as the writing of it has blessed us.

—Mike Nappa, Winter 1999

# 1

*The Fruit of the Spirit Is...*

# $\mathcal{L}$OVE

Imagine, if you will, a world without love of any kind. It's a bleak, desolate world, isn't it? Where there is no love, there is no joy, no satisfaction, no comfort, no home.

But that's not the kind of world God has created—or intended—for us. And so it's no surprise that the first quality listed among the fruit of the Spirit is love, for, as 1 John 4:16 tells us, "God is love."

# A HERO'S LOVE

I keep his picture in my office, in a place where I'll see it every day. It's a picture of Bill Gale. I don't know what he does for a living, or even if he's a Christian. All I really know about him is that he volunteers at a local hospital in the New York City area. Seven years ago I saw his picture in a magazine and he's been my hero ever since.

Let me describe him for you. He's an average-looking man, mid-fifties probably. Narrow shoulders. A hint of pudginess around his middle. Thinnish face. Bald—but denying it by combing a few wispy strands of hair from one side of his head to the other. By all appearances, not really the hero type. But it's what he's doing in that picture that inspires me.

He's holding a baby.

That's it. Nothing more. Just holding a baby. You see, thanks to the mother's drug habit, this infant was born with an addiction to crack cocaine. Doctors say they can't do much for the child—it must break the habit cold turkey.

Where doctors fail, Bill steps in. He can't perform surgery. He can't oversee a blood transfusion. He can't even fill out the hospital forms in triplicate. But he can give a little love to one so helpless it hurts.

Bill cuddles infants. He whispers sweet nothings to them, rocks them, warms them, smiles at them, holds and heals them. They'll never remember Bill, or even know he was there, but he keeps doing it anyway. And because some photographer caught him in the act, I have a picture of what unconditional love looks like.

Every time I gaze at that picture, I see more than just Bill and a baby. I see me—a sin-addicted infant—helpless, in pain, crying for someone to love me. And I see my heavenly Father reaching out to hold me. And I realize Bill Gale is only a dim reflection of the unconditional love that brought Jesus to this earth in the first place, and that made Him willing to die in my place.

That's why Bill Gale is my hero. He reminds me of our eternal Hero's love.

Lavished on me.

## 10 REASONS TO SAY "I LOVE YOU" TO OTHERS

1. Because God said it to you first.

2. Because if you say it enough, people might actually believe it.
3. Because if you don't, they might forget.
4. Because today may be the last time you see them.
5. Because it's a unique opportunity to make someone feel special.
6. Because it makes a heart smile.
7. Because it could prompt someone to say the same to you.
8. Because it's free, but still manages to pays great dividends.
9. Because love is spoken in any language.
10. Because, well. . .because you love them!

☙

## 10 CREATIVE WAYS TO SAY "I LOVE YOU" TO OTHERS

1. Spell it in soap on the bathroom mirror.
2. Sing it into a tape recorder and mail it to someone you love.
3. Write it on the back of a jigsaw puzzle, then give the puzzle to a loved one, saying there's a "secret message" on the back.

4. Write it on a yellow sticky note, then attach the note to your forehead and kiss your spouse so he or she can read it up close.
5. Cut out the words in the shape of a bookmark, and put it in your son or daughter's schoolbook.
6. Write it in sunblock on your shoulder, then lie out until the words show up like a tattoo. Show your sunblock tattoo to loved ones.
7. Hug.
8. Pray.
9. Send a valentine in any month except February. (Might as well send some of those candy hearts too!)
10. Share your chocolate. (Need we say more?)

# 10 WEAK EXCUSES PEOPLE GIVE FOR NOT SAYING "I LOVE YOU" TO OTHERS

1. They already know.
2. I told them once, and I haven't changed my mind yet.

3. I don't like to share my feelings much.
4. They might not love me back.
5. I don't want to embarrass anyone—myself included.
6. Men don't do those kinds of things.
7. I forgot.
8. They should be able to tell by my actions.
9. I'm angry at that person.
10. They never shared chocolate with me.

❧

*Sometimes we substitute our devotion to sinful habits as expressions of love. And, like the man in this story by John Duckworth, we suffer the consequences. . .*

## THE MAN WHO LOVED PORCUPINES

You know the doctor down on Seventh Street? The so-called heart specialist? Yeah, that's the one. If you ever have a problem don't go to see him. The guy's a quack. I mean I went to him with this problem, but he couldn't fix it. Cost me twenty-five bucks to see him, and all he did was throw up his hands as if there were nothing he could do!

It went like this. I sat down on the examination table, and he asked, "So, what seems to be the problem?"

I explained, "Well, doc, I don't know exactly. I keep having these pains in my chest. Shooting pains. Maybe it's my heart."

"Hmm," he muttered. "Take off your shirt, and I'll have a listen."

So I took off my shirt. As soon as I did, this guy just about had a heart attack himself. "Hey!" he said. "What are all those puncture wounds on your chest?"

"Oh, they're nothin'," I breezed.

"Nothing?" he protested. "Son, those are serious wounds. There must be two dozen of them."

"Not counting the ones in my arms," I added.

He looked at my arms and whistled. Then he frowned. "All right," he said. "What happened?"

"Nothin', really. Just a porcupine, that's all."

"A porcupine?" he cried. "Son, to get this many wounds, you'd have to pick up a porcupine with your bare hands and hug it."

"Right," I said. "That's what I did."

He looked at me with a really weird expression. "You hugged a porcupine?" he questioned. "Why would you want to do a thing like that?"

I shrugged. "I'm just into that, I guess. I like porcupines."

He took off his glasses and looked down his nose at me—just like my old man always does. "Son," he said, "you just can't do that. Porcupines aren't good for you. They're dangerous. They can stick you full of quills."

"So?" I said. "Don't knock it until you've tried it."

He shook his head. "I don't have to try it to know it's not good for me. Now promise me you'll stay away from porcupines."

"Hey," I said. "Are you a heart specialist or not? I've got chest pains. What are you going to do about it?"

That's when he threw up his hands. "There's nothing I can do, unless you give up hugging porcupines," he said. Then he put a bandage on my chest and sent me out the door.

Can you believe that guy? I mean, talk about self-righteous! Where does he get off judging my lifestyle? If I want to hug porcupines, that's my business. His job is to get rid of chest pains!

Anyway, I left and went over to the zoo. Sure enough, there were some great porcupines there. I sneaked into the cage, picked one up, and for some reason those chest pains started again. I mean, I thought I was gonna die.

So that's why I'm here, doc. You're a heart specialist, too, right? You've gotta help me. Maybe I need open heart surgery or a transplant or something, huh?

What? You want me to see the guy next door? What kind of doctor is he?

Well, why won't you tell me? What's—

Hey, who are these guys coming through the door? Where are you taking me? I don't want to put on that jacket—

You people are all alike! Trying to crush my alternative lifestyle, imposing your worn-out morality! I'll get you for this! I'll—I'll—

Wait!

I'll. . .uh. . .make you a deal.

No more heart specialists.

How about lots of. . .acupuncture?

# SPEAKING OF LOVE...

"Love alters not with his brief hours and weeks, but bears it out even to the edge of doom."

> —WILLIAM SHAKESPEARE, in *Sonnet 116*

"There are moments, most unexpectedly, when something inside me tries to assure me that. . . love is not the whole of a man's life. . . .Then comes a sudden jab of red-hot memory and all this 'commonsense' vanishes like an ant in the mouth of a furnace."

> —C. S. LEWIS, while mourning the death of his wife in *A Grief Observed*

*"Love is foolish. . . but I still might try it sometime."*

JILL, age 6,
in an Internet posting

"Love doesn't just sit there, like a stone, it has to be made, like bread; re-made all the time, made new."

> —URSULA K. LE GUIN,
> in *The Lathe of Heaven*

"Don't do things like have smelly, green sneakers. You might get attention, but attention ain't the same thing as love."

—ALONZO, age 9,
in another Internet posting

"People who are empty inside and hungry for the love that was denied them in childhood will often risk anything—even the suffering, degradation and death of AIDS—in order to grab just a little fleeting affection."

—KEVIN GRAHAM FORD and JIM DENNEY,
in *Jesus for a New Generation*

*"Hatred paralyzes life; love releases it. Hatred confuses life; love harmonizes it. Hatred darkens life; love illumines it."*

MARTIN LUTHER KING JR.,
in *Strength to Love*

"Many who have spent a lifetime in it can tell us less of love than the child that lost a dog yesterday."

—THORNTON WILDER, as quoted in
*The American Scholar Reader*

"This is true love—a love that continues when we don't feel like it; a love that's unconditional; a love that rejoices in good times and encourages in bad times; a love that lasts forever. That willful, decisive love is what Jesus has for [us]."

—MIKE NAPPA, AMY NAPPA, and MICHAEL WARDEN, in *Get Real*

❧

*Occasionally—no, often—love is a risky business. Mother Teresa proved that time and again, even if it meant risking all to save people some thought were not worth saving. . .*

## IMPOSSIBLE POSSIBILITIES OF LOVE

"Impossible," they said. "You'll be killed!"

But Mother Teresa refused to believe them, and refused to back down.

It was during a time of seemingly endless military conflict in Lebanon. Heavy bombing had trapped thirty-seven "special needs" children in a hospital deep inside the war-torn city of Beirut, Lebanon.

"They are as good as dead," said some.

"Let them die," said others.

Because the fighting still continued, no one was willing to risk an attempt to rescue the children. No one, that is, except Mother Teresa. When she heard of the plight of the thirty-seven, she didn't hesitate.

A frail-looking old woman, Mother Teresa stood only four-feet, eleven-inches tall and weighed less than 100 pounds. But she was a small woman with great love, and she would not sit idly by while these children became just another story of the devastation of war. She determined to let nothing stop her from saving those little ones—not bombs, not guns, and certainly not people telling her it was too risky.

Mother Teresa quickly flew to Beirut and immediately began making arrangements for the rescue. She informed everyone that she would go into the city the next day, "When the fighting stops." It was then she planned to bring out the children.

People looked at her in disbelief, possibly muttering "crazy" under their breath. Love or no love, they knew there'd be no break in the fighting—it had been going on for months! And it seemed that they were right. The fighting continued.

Through the night. Into the morning, bullets and bombs raged until. . .

At precisely the time Mother Teresa had indicated, peace fell over the city. Guns were silent; bombs were held at bay. Unshaken despite the opposition to her cause, Mother Teresa boarded an ambulance, drove deep into the war zone, and brought all thirty-seven children out of danger and into safety. Only after her work was finished did the fighting resume.

Mother Teresa once said, "We can do no great things, only small things with great love." She proved that with her life and her willingness to risk life for the sake of love.

೪

## THE WORD ON LOVE

"Love is patient, love is kind. It does not envy, it does not boast, it is not proud. It is not rude, it is not self-seeking, it is not easily angered, it keeps no record of wrongs. Love does not delight in evil but rejoices with the truth. It always protects, always trusts, always hopes, always perseveres. Love never fails."

—1 Corinthians 13:4–8

"This is love: not that we loved God, but that he loved us and sent his Son as an atoning sacrifice for our sins. Dear friends, since God so loved us, we also ought to love one another. No one has ever seen God; but if we love each other, God lives in us and his love is made complete in us."

—1 John 4:10–12

*"But God demonstrates his*
*own love for us in this:*
*While we were still sinners,*
*Christ died for us."*

Romans 5:8

"The Lord appeared to us in the past, saying: 'I have loved you with an everlasting love; I have drawn you with loving-kindness.' "

—Jeremiah 31:3

"[Jesus said] 'A new command I give you: Love one another. As I have loved you, so you must love one another. All men will know that you are my disciples if you love one another."

—John 13:34–35

# Untitled Poem by
# Michelangelo (1475–1564)[1]

If it be true that any beauteous thing
    Raises the pure and just desire of man
From earth to God, the eternal fount of all,
    Such I believe my love; for as in her
So fair, in whom I all besides forget
    I view the gentle work of her Creator,
I have no care for any other thing
    Whilst thus I love. Nor is it marvelous,
Since the effect is not of my own power,
    If the soul doth by nature, tempted forth,
Enamored through the eyes,
    Repose upon the eyes, which it resembleth,
And through them riseth to the primal love,
    As to its end, and honors in admiring;
For who adores the Maker must love his
    work.

# LOVE SPEAKS TRUE[2]

Ed Rowell, editor for *Leadership* magazine, relates this humorous story about love:

A husband asked his wife, "Tell me, Dear, have you ever been in love before?"

She thought a moment and replied, "No, Darling. I once respected a man for his great intelligence. I admired another for his remarkable courage. I was captivated by yet another for his good looks and charm. But with you, well, how else could you explain it except love?"

# IT'S ALL GREEK TO ME

During the time when the New Testament was written, the Greek language employed many words to describe the different aspects of love. The three most commonly used words, however, were these:

- *Eros*
- *Philia*
- *Agape*

In his excellent resource, the *Expository Dictionary of Bible Words,* theologian Lawrence O. Richards tells more about those Greek terms.

*Eros* embodied the love a man has for a woman and a woman has for a man, explains Richards. That includes sexual desires and physical intimacy. Richards notes that, surprisingly, "This word, much used in Greek culture, is not found in the New Testament."

*Philia,* Richards reveals, was the most common word for love. Though no religious meaning was attached to it in Greek culture, it indicated a "fondness which develops as persons are attracted to each other and build a relationship within or outside the context of family. Loving behavior, which is appropriate between relatives or friends."

*Agape,* (pronounced "Uh-GOP-Ay"), Richards says, "was chosen by the New Testament writers to convey to future generations the unique dimensions and overwhelming depth of God's love and to explore the impact of that love on human beings."

Now, thinking back on your life experience,

which Greek word most describes your experience with love? Which do you most desire to experience? What can you do about that today?

ॐ

## BEDTIME

Last night I went to tuck my son into bed.

I gently arranged the covers, pushed a stray hair out from his eyes,

Leaned close to kiss his cheek and whispered, "I love you."

Instead of saying the same back to me,

He simply smiled and said, "I know."

I paused. How did he know that? I asked.

Rolling his eyes as if I'd asked the dumbest question on earth,

He quickly responded,

"Dad, you tell me that every day. That's how I know."

After a quick hug, I went into the living room.

My wife was reading there.

For no particular reason, I said to her, "I love you."

She simply smiled and said, "I know."

# 2

*The Fruit of the Spirit Is. . .*

# JOY

After years of deep theological study, Bible school degrees, and eons of church attendance, we finally discovered only a few years back something that changed our lives dramatically: God is a joyful Person!

What a difference it makes to know that God is smiling, not frowning, on His children; to know He's preparing a place for us in heaven where we can bask in His joyful presence for all eternity; and to know He has placed a little bit of His joy in our lives today. The real question, then, is: What are we going to do with that joy?

# RECIPE FOR A JOYFUL DAY

Ingredients:
- One relationship with God
- ½ cup gratefulness
- A sprinkling of songs in your heart
- A heaping spoonful of prayer
- A tablespoon of children's giggles
- A dollop of humor
- A dash of sunshine (optional)
- One pair rose-colored glasses (optional)

Lay out one relationship with God as the base. Add gratefulness, songs, and prayer. Mix thoroughly. Next, fold in giggles, humor, and sunshine. Bake overnight with a good night's sleep. Serve with cheerful attitude and joyful determination. Feeds the hungry hearts of one to millions.

# EMPEROR NORTON

Some called him crazy. Others called him a fool. But most San Franciscans in the late 1800s called him Emperor.

Emperor Norton, that is.

His official title was "Emperor of the United States and Protector of Mexico." He "ruled" San Francisco from 1857 to 1880, spreading smiles and joviality. He was just a man with a happy attitude, a merchant who had tried to corner the rice market—and lost his fortune. Yet, after going from riches to poverty, Norton refused to accept that he had to lose his joy. He "crowned" himself and began parading around the streets of San Francisco in full costume as emperor.

There was something so appealing about a man who insisted on enjoying life that the people of the City by the Bay went along with the charade. The good king was granted front row seats at every theater opening. Tailors carefully created and mended his regal plumed hat, cane, and uniform at no cost. The finest restaurants served this monarch their best meals free. The railroads offered transportation "so he could address his subjects." Emperor Norton even had an honorary seat in the state legislature!

How did a man with few financial means earn such a lavish lifestyle? He dealt in a currency that's all too rare—the currency of smiles. His "Majesty" always brought a smile to the faces of others; like the time he ordered a bridge be built to span the bay—the Golden Gate Bridge; or when he decreed that a giant Christmas tree be raised in Union Square for the children of his kingdom.

We can learn a lot from this would-be sovereign. If we would win the hearts of our children, we must be willing to share with them a simple, lasting joy that Jesus gives to life. When we do, our children, like the people of San Francisco, will remember us with fondness.

Funny thing about Emperor Norton. You, too, have probably gotten a little joy from this so-called crazy man. Mark Twain immortalized the emperor in the character of his pauper "king" in the classic novel *The Adventures of Huckleberry Finn*. If you've read the book, you, too, have met the "emperor" of the United States and "protector" of Mexico.

# THE WORD ON JOY

"So I commend the enjoyment of life, because nothing is better for a man under the sun than to eat and drink and be glad."

—Ecclesiastes 8:15

*"A happy heart makes the face cheerful, but heartache crushes the spirit. . . . A cheerful heart is good medicine."*

—Proverbs 15:13, 17:22

"As the Father has loved me, so have I loved you. Now remain in my love. If you obey my commands, you will remain in my love, just as I have obeyed my Father's commands and remain in his love. I have told you this so that my joy may be in you and that your joy may be complete."

—John 15:9–11

"The LORD has done great things for us, and we are filled with joy."

—Psalm 126:3

"This is the day the LORD has made; let us rejoice and be glad in it."

—Psalm 118:24

"The joy of the LORD is your strength."

—Nehemiah 8:10

"Be joyful always."

—1 Thessalonians 5:16

❧

*In his delightfully eloquent book,* Dangerous Wonder, *Michael Yaconelli shares about a time of pure, unadulterated, youthful joy. We enjoyed Michael's joyful reminiscing so much, we had to share it with you here. . .*

## WILD ABANDON

It was the '50s—1952 to be exact. At ten years old, my everyday agenda had one focus—playing. Each day would bring a new challenge as my friends and I determined what activity would capture our attention. We lived in a lower economic neighborhood populated with hundreds of children who never felt poor, never thought about what we didn't have, what we were "deprived" of. We only knew that the options for playing were endless—marbles, street stickball tournaments, Ping-Pong championships, hide-and-seek, squirt-gun fights, swimming at the city pool, riding our bikes to the sugar beet factory, exploring boxcars at isolated train tracks. There were no televisions to distract us (most of our families couldn't afford one), no video games to swallow up the time. All we had was our imaginations.

Looking back at those years, I realize our imaginations were more than enough to keep us busy and make us wish the days were longer. Oh, there were some hot July days in southern California when our energy was sapped and we would complain about "nothing to do." Our parents were not very sympathetic. "There is plenty to do!" they would point out. "And if you can't find anything to do, we have some chores you can do." It didn't take long for us to occupy ourselves.

One July morning as my friends and I were sitting around on our bikes, daydreaming about what might be that day's adventure, Jimmy blurted out, "Let's build a spaceship!" The moment the words left his mouth, we knew destiny had spoken. Three boys on Evergreen Street were to build a spaceship. No one said a word, yet it was clear what we were to do. Our assignments were obvious; we knew instinctively who would do what. Jimmy, the ham operator's son, would be the communications officer and in charge of the radio and engineering components. I was in charge of the spaceship structure—my dad worked at Sears, a great source for rocket shells, otherwise known as refrigerator boxes. Alan was in charge of logistics—his dad was in construction and Alan was very strong. He was also the navigator.

The construction of the spaceship took three full days. My backyard was chosen as the launchpad and subsequent space location, much to my parents' chagrin. It took two days to haul the exterior of the spaceship into place, another day to construct its interior, and then one full day to familiarize ourselves with our new surroundings so that everyone knew his role and was comfortable with his section of the spaceship, and to ensure that all the commands and destinations were mapped out and understood.

We were the envy of the neighborhood, with space voyages occurring daily for weeks. I don't remember how many weeks because, while our spaceship was "operational," we were oblivious to time. Every morning we could hardly wait to get done with our chores and get back in the spaceship. The time went by quickly. For most of the summer our world was our spaceship, where we miraculously survived meteor attacks, intergalactic battles with alien enemies, internal explosions, attempted mutinies, and mysterious forces of evil. There were many other crises we managed to overcome—Jimmy was grounded for a week when it was discovered he had equipped his communications center with his dad's most expensive equipment (after he had spent a week searching his garage for it!). Then there was the rainstorm that weakened the boxes to the point of collapse, followed by the attack of the St. Bernard on the navigator's room. (The navigator was so angry he threatened to quit, so we had to take two days to find a new refrigerator box and help him rebuild his section of the spaceship.)

I'll never forget the day our magical space voyage ended. Apparently, all of our parents met secretly the night before and decided it was time for the spaceship to be dismantled. The lawn under the spaceship was dead, the boxes were caving in after too many dew-filled evenings, and school would be starting in two weeks. We couldn't believe how much debris our spaceship had accumulated over the summer. It took us five full days to rid ourselves of the junk we had collected and to clean up the mess.

What I remember most about my days as captain of our neighborhood spaceship is the wild abandon I experienced. While the spaceship was active, our schedules, our relationships, all of our personal responsibilities fell under the shadow of our imaginary space voyage. Our every waking moment was consumed with the spaceship. By the end of the summer, our parents were frustrated, our friends were angry and jealous, our neighbors were sick of us, and our pets were feeling deprived and rejected because we had ignored them. Our old life had been abandoned for a new life, and we didn't care whether the others thought we used our time wisely or even if they thought we were crazy. We were oblivious to the world around us. It didn't exist. We were children, and for a few short weeks we were allowed to abandon ourselves into the world of our imaginations.

I miss that summer very much. In all the years of my childhood, I was never as alive as I was during those weeks. Every day was vivid, electric, adventurous, invigorating, and exhilarating. Every nerve was standing on tiptoe, every sense was activated, every emotion was alive! My whole being was on call, on alert.

In the summer of 1952, in the unlikely sanctuary of refrigerator and washing machine boxes, I was given my first taste of abandon, my first experience of giving myself over unrestrainedly to an idea larger than myself. God was gifting me, preparing me for that moment when I would bump into Jesus and He would beckon me to come, abandon all else, and follow Him.

⚘

## JOY BREAKS

For some reason a group of friends got into a discussion about humiliating date experiences. Erik took the prize when he told this story:

"My first date with Kim seemed to be ending perfectly," he said. "After a great dinner and stimulating conversation, we found ourselves seated in a romantic spot on a secluded beach watching the ocean waves roll in."

After a moment, Kim said breathlessly, "I

think we should be closer." Erik, surprised and delighted, happily snuggled closer on the blanket and wrapped an arm around her shoulder.

Kim paused for a moment, then said, "I meant to the water."

Years ago, when Mike started applying to colleges, his father urged him to enroll at the father's alma mater. Mike had planned to attend another school, but finally gave in when he was told, "There's a pretty girl behind every tree!"

One semester later, Mike announced in no uncertain terms that he was transferring to another university. When asked to explain why he was leaving, Mike would only reply, "No trees."

We knew our then four-year-old son, Tony, had been watching a little too much TV after joining him for an afternoon of his favorite cartoons. When a commercial for the Sally Jesse Raphael program interrupted his show, he turned to his mother and said with authority, "Mom, that commercial is wrong. It's not Sally, Jesse, and Raphael. The Teenage Mutant Ninja Turtles are Donatello, Michelangelo, Leonardo, and Raphael."

# A Joy-Stealer in the House

Ray could barely contain his excitement. It was Christmas Day, and this nine-year-old boy couldn't wait to tear open those beautifully wrapped presents that bore his name under the tree. Finally, the family was gathered and the joyful celebration began.

Ray quickly grabbed a present, one given to him by his father, and, with childhood expertise, separated the package from its wrapping. Carefully, with anticipation in his heart, he peeled open the box.

Inside was a lump of coal.

Derisive chuckles played accompaniment to Ray's swelling disappointment. Dad had decided to play a gag on his son this year, and he sure thought it was funny.

Ray swallowed hard and tried to keep his spirits up. He reached for another present, also from his father. Enthusiasm tempered a bit, he opened it carefully.

And found yet another piece of coal. Bitterness now replaced the joy Ray had felt only moments earlier. Still, his father laughed.

Unfortunately, the scene repeated itself several times that Christmas morn. Ray's dad had carefully wrapped and placed many presents of coal under the family tree. And each time Ray opened a new lump of coal, he felt the joy of Christmas stolen away from his childlike heart by a Grinch who wore the face of his father.

It's nearly six decades later now. Little Ray has grown up, raised children of his own, served in the military, owned his own business, and finally retired. He has lived a full life and seen many Christmases come and go since the time he was nine. But that coal-filled Christmas remains a vivid memory, and one that still brings pain.

"Dad sure thought that was funny," Ray recalls today, "but, boy, that broke my heart. It hurt this little guy. . . ." Ray's voice trails off, and in an instant you know his father did more than simply play a practical joke on his son. He stole joy from a nine-year-old boy, leaving a scar that still hurts, even sixty years later.

# LAUGHTER: JUST THE FACTS

Scientific studies have shown that:

- Laughter reduces stress.
- Laughter is good exercise, stimulating both abdominal and facial muscles.
- Laughter stimulates the immune system, helping combat colds and other illnesses.
- Laughter is aerobic exercise.
- Laughter strengthens your lungs.
- Laughter releases pleasure-enhancing chemicals in your brain.
- Laughter is an effective treatment for depression.
- A good laugh can be like a good massage, relaxing your muscles from head to toe.
- Laughter stimulates creative thinking.
- Laughter is contagious. Are you a carrier?

# ABCs for Finding Joy in Life

If you're ever having trouble finding that joyful spark to light up your day, try finding it in these twenty-six places:

> Attitude adjustments
> Bible verses
> Chocolate bars
> Digging under a rock (like you did
>     when you were a kid)
> Exercising
> Family photo albums
> Grandma's cookin'
> Heartfelt hugs
> In a good book
> Jesus, the source of true joy
> Kindergarten classes
> Laughable moments
> Music
> Naps
> Ocean waves
> Prayer
> Quiet moments
> Sunrises
> Sunsets
> Toys (electric ones are best!)

Ukulele lessons
Visiting with visitors
Warm puppies
Xanadu-like places
Yard sales
Zoos

## SPEAKING OF JOY. . .

"Too many people think God is sorry He ever invented laughter!"
—The Reverend Kent Hummel,
during a 1998 sermon

"It is the heart that is not yet sure of its God that is afraid to laugh in His presence."
—George MacDonald, in *Sir Gibbie*

"All the world is searching for joy and happiness, but these cannot be purchased for any price in any marketplace, because they are virtues that come from within, and like rare jewels must be polished, for they shine brightest in the light of faith and in the services of brotherly love."
—Lucille R. Taylor, as quoted in
*Relief Society Magazine*

"We have learned that joy is more than a sense of the comic, more than earthly pleasure, and to a believer even more than what we call happiness. Joy is the enjoyment of God and the good things that come from the hand of God. If our new freedom in Christ is a piece of angel food cake, joy is the frosting. If the Bible gives us wonderful words of life, joy supplies the music. If the way to heaven turns out to be an arduous steep climb, joy sets up the chairlift."

—Sherwood Wirt, in *Jesus, Man of Joy*

*"Maybe I'm just a cockeyed optimist, but I think life is to be experienced joyfully rather than endured grudgingly."*

Luci Swindoll, in *We Brake for Joy!*

"The habit of always putting off an experience until you can afford it, or until the time is right, or until you know how to do it is one of the greatest burglars of joy. Be deliberate, but once you've made up your mind—jump in."

—Charles R. Swindoll, in *Living on the Ragged Edge*

"Joy is not found in singing a particular kind of music or in getting with the right kind of group or even in exercising the charismatic gifts of the Spirit, good as all these may be. Joy is found in obedience. When the power that is in Jesus reaches into our work and play and redeems them, there will be joy where once there was mourning."

—Richard J. Foster in
*Celebration of Discipline*

"We must be joyful now. Here. . .within. . . with who we are and what we've got."

—Tim Hansel, in *Holy Sweat*

*"The most destitute person
in the world is
the one without a smile."*

Zig Ziglar,
in *Zig Ziglar's Little Instruction Book*

"How can I be depressed when you keep acting so positive?"

—from a "For Better or For Worse"
cartoon by Lynn Johnston

# A Prayer of
# Saint Teresa of Avila[3]

From silly devotions
and from sour-faced saints,
good Lord, deliver us!

# The Joy Experiments

Experiment #1: Joy Journals

Beginning on a Sunday, chronicle in a notebook or on a yellow legal pad everything that makes you smile. For example, a child's answer in Sunday school, a radiant sunrise, a friend's phone call, a lame joke on late-night TV, a good book, a cozy pet, a lunch with family, a game of football, hot chocolate with marshmallows, a good night's sleep, and so on. Organize your journal by day, and list as many things as you can remember before going to bed.

At the end of your week, review what you've listed and ask yourself these questions:

- What was it about these things that made me smile?
- Why don't I smile more? Or less?
- What can I do this next week to make others smile?
- What do I think makes God smile?

Experiment #2: Overnight Fun-a-Thon

Invite your best friend (a person who may very well be your spouse) to stay up all night on Friday for an overnight Fun-a-Thon. Plan out the whole experience, starting at 10 P.M. Friday and ending at 6 A.M. on Saturday morning. Include anything you two like that makes you laugh, chuckle, smile, or have fun. For example, you might rent a few comedy videos, make a midnight run to the grocery store for chocolate, play goofy games from childhood like Monopoly or Life, practice your karaoke by the stereo, eat more chocolate, invent a bowling alley in your hallway using socks and cola bottles, and, well, you get the idea.

Make the sole purpose of your overnighter simply to have fun and enjoy life with your best friend. When the alarm rings off at 6 A.M., pause for a prayer to thank God for bringing joy into your life, then sleep the day away with a smile on your face.

# 3

*The Fruit of the Spirit Is. . .*

# Peace

In this world of inescapable horrors, sometimes peace seems unattainable, a phantom we glimpse in the distance that evaporates before we arrive.

Then suddenly, unexpectedly, we are treated to a moment that can only be defined as peaceful. The world still rages, sin still wreaks havoc, our problems haven't gone away or lessened, but in that moment we grasp the truth that Jesus Christ, our Prince of Peace, stands alongside as we face the troubles of the day. May one such moment grace your life today.

# On a Quest for Peace[4]

We're told this is a true story, so we present it to you as such. It seems there was once a man who was an officer in the British cavalry. A seasoned soldier, and well-trained, he was sent to serve for England in the Crimean War. There he became a part of history as one of the many ill-fated souls involved in the now-famous "Charge of the Light Brigade."

Fortunately, this soldier survived, but the scars on his soul ever after would not heal. The trauma of being in the midst of such carnage made him long for only one thing: peace.

After the war, this cavalry officer resigned his commission, determined not to face battle or war again. He tried to find peace in his native land, but, disillusioned, finally decided England could no longer be the tranquil home he had once known. It was then he decided to leave his home, to travel across the sea and start anew in the fresh, sun-scrubbed skies of America.

Upon arriving, he began a trek to discover the place that would be his home—a place where peace would reign supreme. By the late 1850s, our hero had found and purchased a small farm in the Virginia countryside that had become all he had hoped for. So, he settled in, ready at last to enjoy the remaining years of his life in peace and tranquility.

There was only one problem. The farm on which he had chosen to retire was in an arca called Bull Run.

ొ

*As a high school social living teacher in California, Nancy Rubin often encouraged her students to write "letters" revealing their thoughts and feelings. For one such assignment a student turned her thoughts to peace and war, and a recent visit to a national monument. . .*

## DEAR VIETNAM WALL[5]

Dear Vietnam Wall,

You are so covered in sorrow that anyone can feel it by a mere glimpse of you. When I saw you I felt so much misery for those who died or are missing, and for those who lost the men engraved in you, that I sat down by your side, and wept quietly for those who cannot. I could not take a single picture of you, because nothing imaginable can capture the incredible emotional experience one experiences at your side. Your picture would have been on the same roll as happy times. You would have made me associate death with cheer and with my friends. You made me think about how insignificant it is to be rich or popular, and cherish the fact that I am alive. I pray that you remain there for centuries to come, to touch other people's souls as you did mine.

—Fifteen-year-old female

❧

## NAME OF JESUS, SOFTLY STEALING[6]
### (Author unknown)

Name of Jesus, softly stealing
    O'er a world of strife and shame,
Thou canst bring us heav'nly healing,
    O Thou all-restoring Name.

Name of Jesus, Heav'n of gladness,
    Cause our doubts and fears to cease;
Soothe away the aching sadness;
    Name of Jesus, give us peace.

# THE WORD ON PEACE

"For unto us a Child is born, Unto us a Son is given; And the government will be upon His shoulder. And His name will be called Wonderful, Counselor, Mighty God, Everlasting Father, Prince of Peace."

—Isaiah 9:6 NKJV

"[Jesus said]
*Peace I leave with you;*
*my peace I give you.*
*I do not give to you as the world gives.*
*Do not let your hearts be troubled*
*and do not be afraid.' "*

John 14:27

"Therefore, since we have been justified through faith, we have peace with God through our Lord Jesus Christ, through whom we have gained access by faith into this grace in which we now stand."

—Romans 5:1–2

"Never pay back evil for evil to anyone. Do things in such a way that everyone can see you are honorable. Do your part to live in peace with everyone, as much as possible. Dear friends, never avenge yourselves. Leave that to God. For it is written, 'I will take vengeance; I will repay those who deserve it,' says the Lord."

—Romans 12:17–19 NLT

"Finally, brothers, good-by. Aim for perfection, listen to my appeal, be of one mind, live in peace. And the God of love and peace will be with you."

—2 Corinthians 13:11

ॐ

## SHALOM!

The Hebrew word for peace used in Scripture is "shalom." Even today, it is commonly used to say good-bye among those of Jewish origin, suggesting that the hearer "go in peace." But, as is always the case when God is involved, there's more to this word than simply a greeting or wish.

Here's how theologian Richard John Neuhaus explains it:

"In both the Hebrew Bible and the New Testament, peace—the *shalom* of God—is tantamount to salvation. It means the bringing together of what was separated, the picking up of the pieces, the healing of the wounds, the fulfillment of the incomplete, the overcoming of the forces of fragmentation by forgiving love. In short, *shalom* is the content of the rule of God, the promised goal of pilgrim hope."

So what kind of *shalom* are you experiencing in life? Perhaps now is a good time to ask God for His *shalom* to reign daily in your life.

⌘

## How Do You Say "Peace"?[7]

In French, you say it "paix."

In Spanish you say it "paz."

In Dutch and Afrikaans you say it "vrede."

In Norwegian you say it "fred."

In Hungarian you say it "béke."

In the Czech language you say it "mír."

In Pig Latin you say it "Eacepay."

At work you say it with a team attitude and in a job well done.

At home you say it with smiles and affection.

At church you say it in the words of the tax collector from Scripture, "God, be merciful to me a sinner!" (Luke 18:13, NKJV)

With enemies you say it in forgiveness.

With loved ones you also say it in forgiveness.

In your heart, you say it by surrender of all to Jesus Christ.

In eternity you say it in a phrase: "Father, I'm home."

❧

## PICTURES OF PEACE

*What symbols do you associate with peace? A dove? A sunset? Two fingers raised in a "V" shape? The ocean? A rainbow? If you'd like to have physical reminders to seek God's peace each day, try your hand at one of these crafty activities:*

*Dove Ornament:* You'll need scissors, a pencil, and one sheet of white posterboard or heavy paper. Trace the outline of a dove onto your paper. Set or hang this little symbol of peace in a place you're not likely to feel peaceful—for example, hang it from the rearview mirror of your car, or set it on your desk at work. Every time you see it, take a moment to ask God to fill your life with His peace—even if someone does cut you off in rush hour traffic.

*Pillow of Peace:* Your level of "craftiness" will determine how detailed this craft is—we suggest you keep it easy so you don't lose peace or patience (that's another chapter) in the process. First choose a symbol that represents peace to you. It could be as intricate as a scenic meadow or as simple as the word "peace." Then create a pillow with this image of peace on it. If you're gifted in sewing, you might embroider or cross-stitch your picture on the face of a pillow you've made by hand. Those a bit less talented can purchase a premade pillow and use fabric paints to re-create their image of peace on the pillow. And if you're hopelessly hindered by anything involving a needle, choose fabric crayons to draw your picture of peace on a premade pillow. When your pillow is finished, use it as a place to rest your head when the worries of the world are stealing peace from your heart.

*Peace Please!* For this simple craft you'll need scissors, light cardboard, a pencil, and the dove you made earlier. Copy the dove onto your cardboard and cut out the shape. This is a small sign you can hang upon your doorknob when you need a few minutes of peace by yourself. You can decorate this placard in any way you like (markers, stickers, doodles) and with any message you like. You might stick with our simple plea of "Peace Please!" or try "Peaceful moment inside—enter quietly," or "Peacefully resting—please don't disturb." Then the next time you're feeling like you could use a few minutes of peace and quiet, hang this notice on your doorknob and close the door. You'll have a few free moments to relax, read, pray, and regain a peaceful heart.

❧

## A Prayer of Martin Luther King Jr. (1956)[8]

O God, our Heavenly Father. . . . Keep us, we pray, in perfect peace, help us to walk together, pray together, sing together, and live together until that day when all God's children, black, white, red, and yellow will rejoice in one common band of humanity in the kingdom of our Lord and of our God, we pray. Amen.

# Peaceful America?[9]

During a 1952 polio epidemic, 3,152 people were killed by the disease. During a 1990 epidemic of gun violence, 37,184 people in the U.S. were killed by gunfire.

- In 1991 alone, 5,356 children were killed by gunshot wounds.

- In 1992, 1,000,000 crimes with guns were recorded, and 13,000 murders by gunfire were committed.

- The United States has the highest homicide rate in the world, fully four times higher than our closest competitor.

- In an average year, nearly 1,000,000 American teenagers are victims of violent crimes.

- A black teenager is six times more likely to be a homicide victim than a white teenager is.

- Today in the U.S., sixty-five men, women, and children will die due to injuries sustained from handgun fire.

# Broken Crosses

As a child in the seventies, I saw a cross,
    upside down and broken, wrapped in
    a circle.
"It's a peace sign," they told me, and I
    tried to believe.
Back then, peace signs spackled across the
    universe,
Sold on T-shirts, necklaces, earrings,
    bandannas, and more.
But the people who held those signs
    always seemed so angry, so ruthless,
    so selfish, so cold.
"That can't be peace," I thought.
As a teenager in the eighties, I saw a
    different cross, this one right side up,
    with a man broken upon it.

"It's Christ," they told me, "and He died
    on the cross to make peace with God
    for you."
Once more, I tried to believe.
It was then I discovered that peace can't be
    found in signs or symbols.
It's not in a necklace or on a T-shirt, or
    pasted to a protester's placard, but in a
    Person, in a relationship,
In the royal family of the Prince of Peace.
Without Him, all we are left with is
    broken crosses, upside down, and
    wrapped in a circle.

# A Prayer of
# Saint Francis of Assisi[10]

Lord, make me an instrument of Your peace.
Where there is hatred, let me sow love;
Where there is injury, pardon;
Where there is doubt, faith;
Where there is despair, hope;
Where there is darkness, light;
Where there is sadness, joy.

*Several years ago, our friends John and Liz Duckworth experienced the heartbreak of losing a newborn child. Katherine Ann Duckworth had the misfortune of being born with a condition called "Trisomy 18"—meaning she was born with a third chromosome. Unfortunately, the condition is almost always fatal.*

*As John and Liz wrestled with the emotions of dealing with this unexpected trauma, they somehow managed to find peace in the midst of sorrow's storm. Listen now as John recounts his experience during the days after Katherine's birth. . .*

## KATHERINE
### by John Duckworth

Tuesday afternoon we almost lose her. The doctor on duty at Loyola calls us at Central DuPage, reporting Katherine has had a bad spell but rallied. Little by little, her heart is beginning to fail. He wants to know: If her heart stops again, do we want CPR performed on her?

Friends are milling around the room, chatting, as I listen to this stranger ask his life-or-death question. I ask the doctor whether resuscitating Katherine would cause her pain. It could, he says. Feeling she has suffered enough, we tell the doctor that if our baby slips away, not to use such measures to bring her back.

It could happen any time now, we realize. Subconsciously we begin to wait for the phone to ring again, this time with a final message.

I go home for awhile, as I have been doing at night and some mealtimes, feeling alien in my own house. I find myself doing what I never do, flipping my Bible open just to see where it lands, hoping it will land in a place that means something right now.

It opens to 2 Corinthians 4:7–9, 12, 16–18 [NIV]:

"But we have this treasure in jars of clay to show that this all-surpassing power is from God and not from us. We are hard pressed on every side, but not crushed; perplexed, but not in despair; persecuted, but not abandoned; struck down, but not destroyed. . . . So then, death is at work in us, but life is at work in you. . . . Therefore we do not lose heart. Though outwardly we are wasting away, yet inwardly we are being renewed day by day. For our light and momentary troubles are achieving for us an eternal glory that far outweighs them all. So we fix our eyes not on what is seen, but on what is unseen. For what is seen is temporary, but what is unseen is eternal."

Late Tuesday afternoon, Liz is released from the hospital. We trace and retrace the forty-five-minute route between our home and Katherine's, spending as much time with her as we can. We hold her for hours, watching the numbers on the monitors climb and plummet. Whenever they dip too low, alarms sound and a nurse comes running. But Katherine stays alive.

She stays Wednesday to hear the lullaby I wrote for her months ago. She stays Thursday to be held by my parents, who have flown in from Oregon to see their first grandchild and embrace us tearfully. . . But she cannot stay forever. . .

It is Friday, 4 P.M.

Liz and I ride the elevator up to the neonatal intensive care unit. Our parents are back at our house, waiting and praying. There is a room at Loyola in which things like this happen, a room next to the one where Katherine lives. It is a small, windowless room with light green walls and two fold-out chairs in which parents can sleep when they are staying the night. It is to this room that Liz and I go.

We sit on fold-out chairs and wait. I have brought a camera. We have learned this week to take as many pictures as we can.

My heart is in my throat as Katherine is brought in. Dr. Muraskas has prepared us for the possibility that she may have only moments left, but to everyone's surprise she is breathing on her own for the first time.

And for the first time, we see her whole face, without tubes or tape. Her tiny mouth is like a jewel, as silent as always, but pink and perfect. She is unfettered now by electrodes and monitors. There are no fluctuating readouts to stare at in this room, no alarms to dread. There is only an IV stand and a tube connected to her foot, through which she receives nourishment.

She wears the smallest outfit we could find, a newborn size T-shirt with a rabbit on it. It looks like a tent on her miniature frame; her weight has dipped to two pounds, fourteen ounces.

The doctor and nurses leave. Liz holds her first, on a pink and blue and white crocheted blanket. I try to keep my hands from shaking as I take one picture after another. A few times Katherine opens her eyes and we say, "Oh, look!" as if we have seen a shooting star or spouting whale, while in reality we have seen something far more special.

I have used up my film. She is still alive.

My heart thunders in my chest as I drop to my knees and pray aloud, knowing that she could be gone by the time I say amen. "Into Your hands we commend her spirit," I pray, the monumental words sticking in my throat.

She is still with us. We take turns holding her and waiting. . .

The hallways of the great hospital are nearly deserted. We find a small room lined with vending machines. We are too tired to say much as we eat a hastily chosen snack.

We return to the room, and Liz sleeps. I hold Katherine, determined not to doze. She appears to be straining now, gasping for breath. Her heart rate is down to a mere seven beats per minute. I beg God to take her home.

Finally my watch says it is morning. Saturday morning, one week after Katherine's birth. Around 7:30 I lie down as Liz holds our little girl.

I close my eyes. When I open them, it is 8:00.

"I think she's gone," Liz says quietly, looking down at the peaceful bundle in her lap.

Dazed, I go out to get the nurse. She gets

Dr. Muraskas, and they come in. The doctor puts his stethoscope to Katherine's tiny chest. We wait for a long time.

At last he speaks. "She's in heaven," he says simply.

We ask for a few more minutes with her, and are left alone. Liz passes the featherweight body to me, and I hold it to my chest, cradling the precious head under my chin. I touch the softness, the wispy hair, the ebbing warmth I must never forget. I draw a deep breath, and a shuddering sob escapes from somewhere deep inside.

And at that moment, in a place so close yet so far away, on the other side of the door that is this room, a little girl is whole and happy, running and dancing in the Light. There are no tears where she is. No seizures, no defects, no gasping for breath.

I hug what she has left behind. I look through bloodshot eyes across the little room at the brave and beautiful woman who has spent this night as I have, peering into the darkness and sensing the radiant welcome of the Light Himself.

And together, without speaking, we fix our eyes on what is unseen, for that is eternal.

It is why, though we are hard pressed on this bleak March morning, we are not crushed.

And it is why, though our sadness seems unbearable, we are convinced as never before that neither death nor life, nor anything else in all creation, can separate us from the love of God that is in Christ Jesus our Lord.

Nor from our daughter, Katherine.

# 4

*The Fruit of the Spirit Is...*

# Patience

Few qualities of Christian virtue are more needed and desired than patience. The only problem is that patience takes time! You cannot slap a frozen dose of patience in the microwave and have it miraculously appear after two-and-a-half minutes (three in higher altitudes). No, like a garden it must grow, planted first in seed, then being nourished to sprout centimeter by centimeter, inch by inch, until it finally reaches full bloom into our lives.

Our hope is that in this chapter you'll find the encouragement you need to nourish your own garden of patience in the days that come.

# A Prayer of William Barclay[11]

O God, my Father, give me patience all
  through today.
Give me patience with my work, so that
  I may work at a job until I finish it
  or get it right, no matter how difficult or boring it may be.
Give me patience with people, so that I
  will not become irritated or
  annoyed, and so that I never lose
  my temper with them.
Give me patience with life, so that I
  may not give up hope when hopes
  are long in coming true; so that I
  may accept disappointment without
  bitterness and delay without com-
  plaint.
Hear this my morning prayer for Your
  love's sake. Amen.

*NFL superstar—and Super Bowl champion— Eugene Robinson patiently endured eleven frustrating years as a professional football player before finally winning "the big one." Listen to his thoughts as he reflects on the time he spent waiting for that crowning achievement:*

## EUGENE ROBINSON: CHAMPION IN WAITING[12]

Just getting to a Super Bowl—much less winning it—takes incredible endurance on the part of every player and coach on the team. I don't care how talented a team is, how overwhelming it is on offense or defense, that team isn't going to get there without endurance.

Personally, I would never have had a chance to play in the Super Bowl had I not been able to endure some tough times in my career. Don't get me wrong, it's been a great ride for me. I've had some frustrating times in my career, but overall I wouldn't have missed it for anything. I have fond memories of my time as a Seattle Seahawk— even of those seasons where we struggled. But I had to endure eleven years in the NFL in order to have my shot at a Super Bowl championship.

It took a great amount of work and personal sacrifice to reach that goal. . .

The rewards for our perseverance, our hard work—our endurance—were great, both from a professional standpoint and from a spiritual one.

❧

*Not knowing how something will end can be so frustrating—especially when there's nothing you can do but wait to see how it turns out! Listen to Amy as she relates what she learned from just such an experience. . .*

## SURPRISE!

On the evening before my thirtieth birthday, I was stunned to see my husband, Mike, come home with another woman. (OK, so she was just our baby-sitter, Nicole, but I was stunned anyway.)

"You're late!" I snapped. "And why is Nicole here? Don't you know we're supposed to be at Steve and Cindy's right now?"

I'd prepared a meal for our friends who had

just had a baby, and Mike knew he was supposed to be home so I could use the car. By the time he arrived (with the other woman!), the dinner was getting cold, my patience had been exhausted, and I'd spent a good twenty minutes fuming around the kitchen.

Mike simply grinned and said, "Surprise!" Then he calmly added, "Go pack a few things. We're going on an adventure and won't be back until tomorrow morning." Next he turned to our son, Tony, to let him know that Nicole would be staying with him while we were gone.

"Hooray!" said Tony. (He loves Nicole.)

"Forget it," said me. And to prove my point, I started to cry. (You know, one of those hard, red-in-the-face kind of cries—the kind usually reserved for hitting your thumb with a hammer.)

"This isn't what I'd planned," I sobbed.

Mike wrapped his arms around me in a comforting hug. "Trust me," he whispered. "OK?" I dried my tears, gathered my clothes, and reluctantly got into the car.

We dropped off the dinner to our friends, and thirty minutes later were ourselves dining at the niccst restaurant in town. And that wasn't all! We headed to a guest ranch in the foothills of the Colorado Rockies. Mike had rented the honeymoon suite of a beautiful cabin on the river. What's more, he'd sneaked up to the cabin early. As a result of his preparations, a romantic evening of chocolates, sparkling cider, and a cozy fire all awaited me. All I needed to do was wait, and trust that he would arrive in time to celebrate my birthday in a special way.

As I look back on that memory of frazzled patience and honeymoon-style surprises, I realize that I'm not the only one who has almost missed out on a blessing because of being too impatient to wait. Two thousand years ago, Jesus' friends (like me) had to wait in the darkness while Christ prepared a surprise. But instead of bringing home a baby-sitter, Jesus went out to meet his death on a cross.

I imagine that as they watched Jesus marching to his execution, Jesus' followers had some of the impatient, angry, frustrated feelings I had.

"God, this isn't what we had planned! What's going on here?"

"Jesus, we've been waiting for you to set up Your kingdom, not leave us stranded while you are beaten like a common criminal!"

"How can this be happening to Him? To me? How will we ever go on?"

And I imagine God gently wrapping up those people in His arms of love and whispering words of comfort like, "Be patient. Wait. Trust me."

I can't help but think when that stone rolled away from the tomb that first Easter morning that Jesus grinned just a bit and said to the world, "Surprise!" And I picture Jesus crying tears of joy with Mary Magdalene when she realized her waiting was over, that her Messiah had returned to life. I think He must've chuckled with delight when Peter ran to the tomb and found only empty burial clothes.

And, most of all, I'm thankful that He's prepared for me much more than a honeymoon suite in the mountains. On that day when He surprised humanity by defeating death, Jesus made it possible for me to go on a lifetime adventure that leads to an eternal, heavenly home.

If you ask me, that home will be worth the wait.

# A Prayer of
# Sir Francis Drake
# (1540–1596)[13]

O Lord God, when you give to your servants to endeavor any great matter, grant us also to know that it is not the beginning, but the continuing of the same until it be thoroughly finished which yields the true glory.

*Two classic fables from Aesop teach us much about the value of patience, so we include for you here* The Hare and the Tortoise, *and* The Goose with the Golden Eggs.

## The Hare and
## the Tortoise

by Aesop

A Hare was once boasting about how fast he could run when a Tortoise, overhearing him, said, "I'll run you a race."

"Done," said the Hare and laughed to himself. "But let's get the Fox for a judge."

The Fox consented and the two started. The Hare quickly outran the Tortoise, and knowing he was far ahead, lay down to take a nap. "I can soon pass the Tortoise whenever I awaken." But unfortunately, the Hare overslept himself. Therefore, when he awoke, though he ran his best, he found the Tortoise was already at the goal.

He learned that "Slow and steady wins the race."

## THE GOOSE WITH THE GOLDEN EGGS

by Aesop

Once upon a time a Man had a Goose that laid a Golden Egg every day. Although he was gradually becoming rich, he grew impatient. He wanted to get all his treasure at once. Therefore, he killed the Goose. Cutting her open, he found her just like any other goose, and he learned to his sorrow that "It takes time to win success."

# Ten Patience-Enhancers for Everyday Life

Next time you're feeling stressed and your patience is waning, try one of these quick "patience-enhancers" to help reclaim your calm:

1. Pray.
2. Breathe deeply and think of sunsets.
3. Remember God's incredible patience toward you.
4. Eat chocolate. (Might not help, but it'll still taste good!)
5. Pray some more.
6. Give yourself a "time out" and spend ten minutes alone.
7. Read 2 Peter 3:8–9.
8. Put yourself in another person's circumstances.
9. Think eternally. (Is this really going to matter in the long run?)
10. Pray! Pray! Pray!

# THEOLOGIAN LAWRENCE O. RICHARDS ON PATIENCE[14]:

The New Testament contains many exhortations to be patient. But just what is patience? The Greek word (*makrothymeo/makrothymia*) focuses our attention on restraint: that capacity for self-control despite circumstances that might arouse our passions or cause agitation. In personal relationships, patience is forbearance. This is not so much a trait as a way of life. We keep on loving or forgiving despite provocation, as illustrated in Jesus' pointed stories in Matthew 18. Patience also has to do with our reaction to the troubles we experience in life.

*The Bible records the story of Job, a man who, in spite of enduring a host of horrible physical and emotional trials, patiently refused to give up on God. In his beautiful work,* The Book of Beginnings, *Dr. Steve Stephens imagines what it might have been like to witness the patient struggles of Job. Listen as he retells a portion of that ancient story here. . .*

## THE LAND BARON

Land-Baron could find no comfort. When exhaustion overwhelmed him, night terrors taunted his sleep. During the day unrestrained itching left him crazed. His legs grew thick and swollen until his knees and ankles could not be distinguished. His hard skin cracked and ulcerated, seeping onto the strips of cloth that served as bandages.

The stench forced his wife to keep her distance.

Children stared.

Adults turned their eyes away.

Even the village healer held his breath when he examined the wounds. The healer took Land-Baron's wife aside.

"I wish there was something I could give, but I can do nothing even to ease his suffering. We must protect the village from this horrid sickness. Land-Baron must live in isolation outside the village."

"Must I go with him? Why should I have to suffer because of his disease? Why don't his brothers and sisters take care of him?"

"Your husband will not live long. Try to make his final days comfortable."

That afternoon, Land-Baron moved outside the village. Every step was painful and not even his wife would touch him to help. But his cracked and bleeding lips never complained. He carried his revolting body with a grace.

"Aren't you angry at the Garden-Maker?" His wife spit the words into his face. "Look what you get for all your efforts to be his friend and walk with him."

"I didn't walk with the Garden-Maker to get anything. I did it because of who he is."

"A liar he is. The sky banner to remind us of his care? Look at what he does to his most faithful. He shouldn't care so much."

"There is a reason for all I don't understand. Garden-Maker has an intent. I know he does."

"You pathetic optimist. Cry out to Garden-Maker until you lose your voice. If I were you, I'd curse his name and die."

Land-Baron was silent as he sat in the dusty heat and gritted his teeth against the torment. His wife shook her head and walked back to the village. . .

*In spite of the fact that he had now lost everything, Job patiently endured his suffering—so much so that he has since become the ultimate example of human patience, even inspiring the compliment "He (or she) has the patience of Job!"*

*Curious how Job's patience was rewarded? Read chapter 42 of the book of Job in the Bible to find out for yourself!*

# THE WORD ON PATIENCE

"The end of a matter is better than its beginning, and patience is better than pride. Do not be quickly provoked in your spirit, for anger resides in the lap of fools."

—Ecclesiastes 7:8–9

"Here is a trustworthy saying that deserves full acceptance: Christ Jesus came into the world to save sinners—of whom I am the worst. But for that very reason I was shown mercy so that in me, the worst of sinners, Christ Jesus might display his unlimited patience as an example for those who would believe on him and receive eternal life."

—1 Timothy 1:15–16

"Bear in mind that our Lord's patience means salvation, just as our dear brother Paul also wrote you with the wisdom that God gave him."

—2 Peter 3:15

"Now may the God of patience and comfort grant you to be like-minded toward one another, according to Christ Jesus, that you may with one mind and one mouth glorify the God and Father of our Lord Jesus Christ."

—Romans 15:5–6 NKJV

"Dear brothers and sisters, you must be patient as you wait for the Lord's return. Consider the farmers who eagerly look for the rains in the fall and in the spring. They patiently wait for the precious harvest to ripen. You, too, must be patient. And take courage, for the coming of the Lord is near.

"Don't grumble about each other, my brothers and sisters, or God will judge you. For look! The great Judge is coming. He is standing at the door!

"For examples of patience in suffering, dear brothers and sisters, look at the prophets who spoke in the name of the Lord. We give great honor to those who endure under suffering. Job is an example of a man who endured patiently. From his experience we see how the Lord's plan finally ended in good, for he is full of tenderness and mercy."

—James 5:7–11 NLT

*Sometimes the most difficult person to be patient with is God Himself! Once, after feeling the frustration of seemingly unanswered prayers, Mike wrote this essay he titled:*

# I Prayed.
# Nothing Happened.
# Now What?

I once challenged an atheist to pray this simple prayer for seven days: "God, show me the value of prayer. Amen." My "atheist" friend refused the challenge. He was afraid of what might happen. He was worried his prayer might be answered! Then he'd have to change his carefully thought out disbelief—and he didn't want to give God that chance.

Since 95 percent of Americans have experienced answers to prayer[15], that poor atheist had reason to be concerned. Even though he couldn't intellectually admit the existence of God, the truth remains that God does exist and He does answer prayers.

Like the time Reggie White prayed that God would heal torn ligaments in his knee in time for him to play in an important football game for the Green Bay Packers. (God healed him.)[16]

Or the time my church prayed for a boy named Trent. Doctors had discovered an *enormous* blood clot that ran from his leg up into his torso, and they were unable to treat it completely. People in our church took shifts praying for twenty-four hours straight. Next time he went to the doctor, that huge clot was 90 percent gone. Soon after, it disappeared entirely.

When I think of stories like that, sometimes it makes me wonder what I've been doing wrong. Because I know God *does* answer prayer, it makes it all the more frustrating for me when my own prayers *aren't*—and unfortunately that happens more often than I'd like to admit.

I prayed for Nina Brooks for a while. Like Trent, she was a much-loved member of our congregation. She was the sister-in-law of our associate pastor, and a loving wife and mother. And she had a deteriorating liver that was killing her. Her only hope was a liver transplant, but years passed and no liver was available for her.

Nina's condition became critical. The hospital searched frantically for a liver to transplant. And we prayed. Boy, did we pray! Our entire church prayed for weeks, then months, for this woman—much longer than we'd prayed for Trent. Nina slipped in and out of a coma. Then, in spite of our prayers, she died in a hospital bed.

I've found that I'm not the only one whose prayers sometimes go unanswered.

Jeff was in college and a leader in his church's college group when he prayed, "God, let me feel You. Give me some kind of feeling of You to help me know You're real."

Then he waited.

And waited.

And waited some more. Finally, Jeff quit waiting, quit going to church, quit reading his Bible, and quit praying. He never got that "feeling" of God's presence, so he turned his back on Christianity and moved on to something else.

Isaac is a junior in high school. A few years ago, his family took a big leap and opened a small Italian restaurant in town. It was a great hit! Everyone who ate there loved it, and it got excellent word-of-mouth reviews all over town. The only trouble was it wasn't making any money.

Isaac's family poured everything they had into the restaurant. Isaac even worked in the kitchen and filled in as a busboy. All the while Isaac and his family prayed for God to meet the financial needs of the restaurant and their family.

They lasted about a year and a half, then had to file for bankruptcy, sell their house and car to pay as much of their debt as possible, and close the restaurant doors. Isaac's dad now works as a glass installer, and Isaac doesn't understand why God didn't answer their prayers.

At times like these my patience with God wears thin. My soul screams, "God, we prayed! Nothing happened! Now what?" I can't understand why God would work a miracle so Reggie White could play in a football game, and yet do what seems like nothing when the mother of teenagers in my church is left to die, or when a young man turns from God, or when a teenager sees his family go bankrupt.

Oh, I've heard all the standard answers: "Remember, God answers prayers sometimes yes, sometimes no, and sometimes maybe so!" "Remember, God's timing isn't the same as ours!" "Remember, God's going to bring something even better into your life!"

And I've heard all the standard excuses: "You didn't pray long enough." "You didn't pray sincerely enough." "Your prayer was a selfish one." "You must have some sin in your life that blocked your prayer."

Somehow, none of these standard comments give me much comfort—and I'm betting they don't do much for you and Nina Brooks's children either.

So what do I do? I prayed, nothing happened. Now what? It helps me to remember some things.

First, I remember that I'm not alone. In fact, like me (and maybe you too!) Jesus felt the pain of a seemingly unanswered prayer. The Bible reveals in Matthew 26:36–46 that Jesus prayed for deliverance from a "cup of suffering"—that is, His impending death on the cross. (Come to think of it, I'd pray for deliverance from that too!) That request was left unanswered, and Jesus died brutally. . .

. . .then returned to life again having defeated the power of sin and death. Because of that I now have the privilege of knowing God— and praying to Him!

I also remember that God does answer my prayers, just not always in ways that I notice or fully understand. Sometimes instead of asking "Did God answer my prayer?" I need to ask,

"*How* did God answer my prayer?" I prayed for Nina Brooks to be healed. Maybe God's answer in that situation was to bring Nina into His heavenly kingdom where He could give her a new body that's healed for eternity. (See 1 Thessalonians 4:13–18 and Philippians 3:20–21.)

And I remember that prayer isn't just a spiritual version of Santa's toy sack. God never intended my prayers to be wish lists filled solely with my requests for what I think I need. Rather, prayer is a vehicle by which I can miraculously pursue intimacy with the all-powerful God.

So, in that sense, I suppose *something* happens every time I pray. I make contact with eternity. I get a chance to let God know how I feel, to laugh and cry in my Father's presence, and to trust God no matter how life's circumstances turn out.

Perhaps instead of whining, "I prayed, nothing happened," I need to learn how to simply say, "I prayed. That's enough."

Maybe you need to learn that too.

*Perhaps the greatest example of patience is seen in the parable Jesus told of the Prodigal Son. As you read it below, remember that, like the father in this parable, God still waits for you to come home too.*

## THE PRODIGAL SON
## (LUKE 15:11–32 NLT)

To illustrate the point further, Jesus told them this story: "A man had two sons. The younger son told his father, 'I want my share of your estate now, instead of waiting until you die.' So his father agreed to divide his wealth between his sons.

"A few days later this younger son packed all his belongings and took a trip to a distant land, and there he wasted all his money on wild living. About the time his money ran out, a great famine swept over the land, and he began to starve. He persuaded a local farmer to hire him to feed his pigs. The boy became so hungry that even the pods he was feeding the pigs looked good to him. But no one gave him anything.

"When he finally came to his senses, he said to himself, 'At home even the hired men have food enough to spare, and here I am, dying of hunger! I will go home to my father and say, "Father, I have sinned against both heaven and you, and I am no longer worthy of being called your son. Please take me on as a hired man.'"

"So he returned home to his father. And while he was still a long distance away, his father saw him coming. Filled with love and compassion, he ran to his son, embraced him, and kissed him. His son said to him, 'Father, I have sinned against both heaven and you, and I am no longer worthy of being called your son.'

"But his father said to the servants, 'Quick! Bring the finest robe in the house and put it on him. Get a ring for his finger, and sandals for his feet. And kill the calf we have been fattening in the pen. We must celebrate with a feast, for this son of mine was dead and has now returned to life. He was lost, but now he is found.' So the party began.

"Meanwhile, the older son was in the fields working. When he returned home, he heard music and dancing in the house, and he asked one of the servants what was going on. 'Your brother is back,' he was told, 'and your father has killed the calf we were fattening and has prepared a great feast. We are celebrating because of his safe return.'

"The older brother was angry and wouldn't go in. His father came out and begged him, but he replied, 'All these years I've worked hard for you and never once refused to do a single thing you told me to. And in all that time you never gave me even one young goat for a feast with my friends. Yet when this son of yours comes back after squandering your money on prostitutes, you celebrate by killing the finest calf we have.'

"His father said to him, 'Look, dear son, you and I are very close, and everything I have is yours. We had to celebrate this happy day. For your brother was dead and has come back to life! He was lost, but now he is found!' "

# 5

*The Fruit of the Spirit Is. . .*

# Kindness

Pause for a moment right now and answer this question: What is the greatest act of kindness you've ever received from someone? Was it the compassion of a mother? The support of a friend? The encouragement of a neighbor? The generosity of a stranger?

Whatever it was, chances are it not only enriched your life, but made the world a better place for others as well. That's because, like basic mathematics, kindness multiplies, spreading from you to others, who in turn continue spreading it across the globe. May this chapter encourage you to be a multiplier of kindness in the lives of others today, because if it does, we all will feel the benefit.

# Novel Advice[17]

*Classic American novelist, Henry James, was once saying good-bye to his nephew, Willie. Wishing to give the boy his best parting words of advice, Uncle Henry said this:*

"Willie, there are three things that are important in human life. The first is to be kind. The second is to be kind. The third is to be kind."

⟡

# If I Can Stop One Heart from Breaking[18]
by Emily Dickinson

If I can stop one heart from breaking,
    I shall not live in vain;
If I can ease one life the aching,
    Or cool one pain,
Or help one fainting robin
    Unto his nest again,
I shall not live in vain.

# COMPASSION
by Dr. Harold J. Sala

World War II was winding down when Bob Pierce visited a mission school and orphanage run by a group of German sisters near the Tibetan border. While he was there, Pierce noticed a little girl hunched at the bottom of the cold, stone steps. The little girl was obviously undernourished and lacked proper clothing for the cold climate. The child could not have been more than nine or ten, yet her gaunt little face and coal-black eyes reflected as much suffering as some endure in a lifetime.

Deeply concerned, Pierce asked one of the sisters about her. "Oh," she replied, "she comes and sits there every day. She wants to come to school. But we have no room."

The reply did not satisfy him, so he said, "Surely one child won't make that much difference. If she wants to come so badly, could you not make room for just one more?"

The sister turned to Pierce and said, "We have made room for 'just one more' time and time again. We have already four times the number of children we were originally prepared to care for. We have stretched our food as far as it will go. I myself am feeding three others out of my rice bowl, as are all the other sisters. If we do not draw the line somewhere, there will not be enough rice to keep the children we already have alive. We simply cannot take one more child!"

The brutal reality of the situation hit home, but Pierce did not want to accept it. "That is crazy, ridiculous!" he said. "A child cannot come asking for help and be turned away at the door. Why isn't something being done?"

Without saying anything, the sister walked over and swooped the little girl up in her arms. Walking over to Pierce, she deposited the girl in his strong arms and said, "What are you going to do about it?"

That incident led to the founding of World Vision—an organization that has helped feed and clothe thousands of boys and girls. Pierce did what I think you would have done. He dug into his own pocket and gave the sister enough money to buy rice for the little girl. . .

A sister's question founded a great organization. "What are you going to do about it?" It is the question every person must face. When you think of the needs of all the world, you are overwhelmed, but if you can think of the one person outside your gate and face the question, "What am I going to do about it?" you will find that the darkness is driven back at least one step. The needs of people come one at a time; eventually every person must answer the question: "What am I going to do about it?"

✒

## TEN RANDOM ACTS OF KINDNESS YOU CAN DO THIS WEEK

1. Scratch or massage a family member's back.
2. Serenade your mother (she won't mind if you're a little off-key).
3. Leave coins for kids in gumball machines.
4. Let someone behind you in line go ahead of you.
5. Buy lunch for the car behind you in the fast-food drive-thru lane.
6. Compliment every person you come in contact with during a day.
7. Tell someone the good news of Jesus' death and resurrection.

8. Write thank-you cards to your friends just to tell them you appreciate their friendship.
9. Laugh at someone else's jokes.
10. Share your chocolate (OK, just a small piece).

ℰ

*The extraordinary kindness of Mother Teresa toward the sick and dying of the world still stands as a monument years after her death. What was her secret? Perhaps it was in this prayer that she prayed every day:*

# A PRAYER OF MOTHER TERESA OF CALCUTTA, INDIA[19]

Dearest Lord, may I see you today and every day in the person of your sick, and whilst nursing them minister to you.

Though you hide yourself behind the unattractive disguise of the irritable, the exacting, the unreasonable, may I still recognize you and say

"Jesu, my patient, how sweet it is to serve you."

Lord, give me this seeing faith, then my work will never be monotonous. I will ever find joy in humoring the fancies and gratifying the wishes of all poor sufferers.

O beloved sick, how doubly dear you are to me, when you personify Christ; and what a privilege is mine to be allowed to tend you.

Sweetest Lord, make me appreciative of the dignity of my high vocation and its many responsibilities. Never permit me to disgrace it by giving way to coldness, unkindness, or impatience.

And, O God, while you are Jesus my patient, deign also to be to me a patient Jesus, bearing with my faults, looking only to my intention, which is to love and serve you in the person of each of your sick.

Lord, increase my faith, bless my effort and work, now and for evermore.

# KESHIA, KINDNESS, AND THE KKK[20]

Eighteen-year-old Keshia Thomas awoke with a purpose on her mind that warm summer day in 1996. This was the day the infamous Ku Klux Klan was holding a rally near her home in Ann Arbor, Michigan. Many people who opposed the Klan's racist views had planned to gather and march in protest of the organization. A young black woman herself, Keshia was determined to join them.

The protest started off peacefully as crowds of people flooded the streets, waving signs, singing, and shouting to the opposition. Suddenly, almost from nowhere, a white man appeared and flaunted his T-shirt which supported racism and praised the efforts of the KKK. At first people passed him by, but before long his obnoxious sneer and taunting apparel angered many of Keshia's fellow demonstrators.

Without warning, several protesters surged from the ranks of the march and surrounded the lone KKK supporter. Deluging him with kicks, fists, and signs, they quickly overpowered the white man, knocking him down and angrily beating him while he was on the ground.

Nearby, Keshia watched in horror as the terrible unkindness of the KKK supporter sparked an even greater unkindness in the demonstrators. In a selfless act of kindness for her "enemy"—and risking injury herself—Keshia flung herself into the fray. Shouting for the crowd to stop, she dropped to the ground and covered the man, using her own body as a shield to protect him from further injury.

The stunned crowd was silent for a moment. Then, one by one, they slowly rejoined the march and walked harmlessly away. Keshia's risky act of kindness toward an enemy had saved the man—and the day.

❧

## THE WORD ON KINDNESS

"Blessed be the LORD, For He has shown me His marvelous kindness in a strong city!"
—Psalm 31:21 NKJV

"Be kind and compassionate to one another, forgiving each other, just as in Christ God forgave you."
—Ephesians 4:32

"Therefore, as God's chosen people, holy and dearly loved, clothe yourselves with compassion, kindness, humility, gentleness and patience. Bear with each other and forgive whatever grievances you may have against one another. Forgive as the Lord forgave you."

—Colossians 3:12–13

*"What is desirable
in a man is
his kindness."*

Proverbs 19:22 NASB

"Make sure that nobody pays back wrong for wrong, but always try to be kind to each other and to everyone else."

—1 Thessalonians 5:15

# A KIND WORD?

The old joke goes something like this:

A man was on a business trip away from

home at Thanksgiving, and unable to get back in time to spend the holiday with his family. Discouraged and missing his wife and children, he stopped at a diner to eat his lonely Thanksgiving dinner.

"What'll you have?" the waitress asked.

"Just a slice of pumpkin pie and a few kind words," he replied.

Soon after, the waitress returned, placed his order on the table, and turned to walk away.

"Wait a minute!" the man called. "What about my kind words?"

Checking to make sure the cook was out of earshot, the waitress leaned over and whispered, "Don't eat the pie."

❧

## TEN RULES FOR GETTING RID OF THE BLUES[21]
by James S. Hewett

Ten rules for getting rid of the blues: Go out and do something for someone else, and repeat it nine times.

*The ultimate act of kindness is the one we often have the most difficulty with: forgiveness. We would do well to learn from the example of Corrie Ten Boom. . .*

## A LETTER FROM CORRIE TEN BOOM TO THE MAN WHO BETRAYED HER FAMILY TO THE NAZIS[22]

Today I heard that most probably you are the one who betrayed me. I went through ten months of concentration camp. My father died after nine days of imprisonment. My sister died in prison too.

The harm you planned was turned into good for me by God. I came nearer to Him. A severe punishment is awaiting you. I have prayed for you, that the Lord may accept you if you will repent. Think that the Lord Jesus on the Cross also took your sins upon Himself. If you accept this and want to be His child, you are saved for eternity.

I have forgiven you everything. God will

also forgive you everything, if you ask Him. He loves you and He Himself sent His Son to earth to reconcile your sins, which meant to suffer the punishment for you and me. You, on your part have to give an answer to this. If He says: "Come unto Me, give Me your heart," then your answer must be: "Yes, Lord, I come, make me your child." If it is difficult for you to pray, then ask if God will give you His Spirit, who works the faith in your heart.

Never doubt the Lord Jesus' love. He is standing with His arms spread out to receive you. I hope that the path which you will now take may work for your eternal salvation.

❧

## An Unforgiving Servant (Matthew 18:21–35 ncv)

Then Peter came to Jesus and asked, "Lord, when my fellow believer sins against me, how many times must I forgive him? Should I forgive him as many as seven times?"

Jesus answered, "I tell you, you must forgive him more than seven times. You must forgive him even if he does wrong to you seventy-seven times.

"The kingdom of heaven is like a king who decided to collect the money his servants owed him. When the king began to collect his money, a servant who owed him several million dollars was brought to him. But the servant did not have enough money to pay his master, the king. So the master ordered that everything the servant owned should be sold, even the servant's wife and children. Then the money would be used to pay the king what the servant owed.

"But the servant fell on his knees and begged, 'Be patient with me, and I will pay you everything I owe.' The master felt sorry for his servant and told him he did not have to pay it back. Then he let the servant go free.

"Later, that same servant found another servant who owed him a few dollars. The servant grabbed him around the neck and said, 'Pay me the money you owe me!'

"The other servant fell on his knees and begged him, 'Be patient with me, and I will pay you everything I owe.'

"But the first servant refused to be patient. He threw the other servant into prison until he could pay everything he owed. When the other servants saw what had happened, they were very sorry. So they went and told their master all that had happened.

"Then the master called his servant in and said, 'You evil servant! Because you begged me to forget what you owed, I told you that you did not have to pay anything. You should have showed mercy to that other servant, just as I showed mercy to you.' The master was very angry and put the servant in prison to be punished until he could pay everything he owed.

"This king did what my heavenly Father will do to you if you do not forgive your brother or sister from your heart."

*In his play,* Debtor's Prison, *our friend Paul Lessard has written a beautiful allegory of Christ's kindness to us—and our response to Him. We're honored and grateful to be able to include Paul's dramatic expertise as the closing for this chapter.*

# DEBTOR'S PRISON
by Paul Neale Lessard

Summary: Three men are in debtor's prison. In three scenes we hear their stories and come to an understanding of our own positions as debtors before God.

## CHARACTERS
*Duncan*—A longtime resident of the prison, he is hard and gruff, aloof, always cool and unflustered.

*William*—Another longtime resident, he shows more emotion and is somewhat softer than Duncan.

*Terry*—A newcomer to the prison.

*Prison Guard*

*Narrator*—Person offstage who introduces the scenes.

A prison cell. One-inch dowels of varying lengths, painted black, and nailed to a 2 x 6-inch board placed across the front of the stage (downstage right and left) will serve as a grim reminder of the location. Downstage center is where the bench should sit. A table and two chairs are set stage right and a bunk bed is set at an angle, opening up to the audience, just to the left of center stage.

## THE SCRIPT
### "DEBTOR'S PRISON"
### SCENE 1

(As the audience arrives, have a cassette of blues-type music playing in the background. Reserve a seat in the middle of the auditorium for Terry. When it's time for the show to begin, fade out the music and bring up the lights on Duncan and William playing Checkers. Terry enters, wearing drab, tattered clothing and carrying a rolled-up blanket, and sits in the reserved seat.)

*Narrator:* (Offstage) In mid-18th century
England, Europe, and even in Colonial

America, it was not uncommon for men to be imprisoned with no hope of release as a result of bad debts. To be consigned to a debtor's prison, as it was called, was to be forever condemned.

*William:* (Sits up suddenly and moves a checker, jumping three of his opponent's checkers.) Ha! King me!

*Duncan:* (Waving his fist in William's face) I'll king you all right.

*William:* (Pointing at the board) C'mon Duncan, king me. I didn't even cheat this time.

*Duncan:* (Disgusted) After all these games, you finally admit you cheat?

*William:* (Ignoring Duncan's comment) Right here, make this checker a king.

*Duncan:* (Reluctantly crowning the checker) Just because you're getting the first king doesn't mean you've won the game.

*William:* (Gleefully) Not yet, anyway!

(They continue to play, absorbed in the game. At this point the guard enters from the back of the auditorium carrying a dirty piece of paper. It has a list of names with descriptions on it. He stops about halfway up, looks around, spots Terry, and comes to the end of Terry's row. He looks back at his paper and then up at Terry, points to him, and motions for him to come. Terry slowly stands up, looks helplessly around, and points to his chest. The guard nods. Terry, looking defeated, makes his way to the guard, who then escorts him to the stage. No words are exchanged. Escorted by the guard, Terry enters stage right behind the table. The guard then leaves. Terry looks at the two men, who seem oblivious to his presence, and then crosses to the bottom bunk to put his blanket there.)

*Duncan:* (Without looking up) I wouldn't put anything there if I were you.
(Terry stops, straightens up, and reaches to put the blanket on the top bunk.)
*William:* (Clears his throat.) Ahem. . .
(Terry stops once again and turns around to face the men, who still don't look up.)
*Duncan:* (As he moves a checker) I should think this one can sleep on the bench. What do you think, William?
*William:* Suits me fine. Under the window, maybe?
*Duncan:* (With an air of finality) Under the window on the bench.

*William:* It's best really; the last chap didn't last too long sleeping on the floor.

(Terry slowly crosses and places his blanket on the bench. He takes off his jacket and puts it on top of his blanket.)

*Terry:* It doesn't much matter where I sleep. I won't be here long.

*William:* (With mock amazement) Won't be here long? (They both turn to look at Terry.) Don't you know where you are, boy?

*Terry:* Sure I do; I'm not a fool.

*Duncan:* (Back to his Checkers game) Then don't talk like one.

*William:* This is the Dunsmire Debtor's Prison.

*Duncan and William:* (In unison) No one ever leaves.

*Terry:* No one?

*Duncan:* (Contemplating his next move) At least not alive.

*Terry:* (Disbelieving) What? Are you telling me that no one ever pays off their debts?

*Duncan:* (Looking at Terry) If you couldn't take care of your debts on the outside, what makes you think you'll be able to do it in here?

*Terry:* The jailer said that I could work off my debt.

*Duncan:* Don't build your hopes on a jailer's empty promise.

*William:* From our first day, we both tried to work our way out of this prison. It makes the most sense at the start. But after a while you come to realize that you owe so much and you earn so little.

*Duncan:* (Back to his Checkers, shaking his head) I'm surrounded by naive fools.

*Terry:* But my family! I have to get out. My wife and children cannot live with my brother the rest of their lives. (Pause) All it took was two bad crop years, and I was unable to pay the rent on the land we farmed. We had nothing to eat; how could they expect me to pay any rent? If only he could've given me another chance. (Turning away) I'm not a bad person.

*Duncan:* (Sharply) None of us is. It's just not enough to be good. You didn't measure up financially. None of us did, or we wouldn't be here.

*William:* (Wishfully, playing an invisible violin) I had a music shop. Violins, violas, cellos, and double basses. (Looking at his hands) I made instruments that brought music to the whole of England. And

Duncan, well, he was a baker. His pastries, buns, and sweetmeats were the talk of Surrey. What did you call your bakery, Duncan?

*Duncan:* Duncan's Doughnuts.

*William:* He was famous even in London, where I lived.

*Terry:* I'm a farmer. Or was. . .

*William:* Well, you can learn another trade here. Like making shoes,

*Duncan:* or saddles,

*William:* or baking,

*Duncan:* or games of Checkers,

*William:* or license plates.

*Duncan and Terry:* License plates?

*William:* It's experimental. No one really knows what they're for. (Shrugs) But, same as you, we fell upon hard times and were unable to pay our creditors, so we ended up in here.

*Terry:* (Kneels beside his blanket and begins to arrange it like a bed on the bench.) Well, I'll not be in here long. If I work hard and long enough, I know I can pay off my debts and get out of here!

*William:* (Nodding his head slowly) I wish it were true.

(Silence as Terry arranges his bed.)

*Duncan:* (Jumping two checkers) King me. It's your turn, William, but I believe the game may be mine this time.

*William:* (Turning back to the game) Maybe, but I'm still ahead of you 2,346 games to 1,998.

*Duncan:* So you've had a couple of good years. I've got plenty of time to catch up.

(Fade to black. Fade in blues music while stage is dark. Fade out blues as lights come up for Scene 2.)

## SCENE 2

*Narrator:* (Offstage) Terry committed himself to working hard. It was not uncommon for him to put in 15- or 16-hour days, seven days a week in his efforts to pay off the debt that led to his imprisonment. Finally, after his first full year in the Dunsmire Debtor's Prison, he asked the jailer for a review of his work. Terry wanted to know how far along he was in paying off his debt.

(Scene opens with Duncan and William playing Checkers again. However, William is lying on the top bunk, with his hand under his head, looking at the ceiling and humming. Duncan is engrossed in the game. He has only one red checker left, and the black checkers are doubled—all William's pieces are kings. Duncan is making blowing noises in his frustration as he tries to figure out his next move.)

*William:* Give up, Duncan.
*Duncan:* Never!
*William:* (Sitting up on one elbow) You have one checker left. I have all kings. Admit it, you're defeated.
*Duncan:* More time—I need more time.
*William:* Well, that's the one thing I do have plenty of. . .
(Terry walks in slowly. He's wearing a very worn bandanna around his neck. He sits down in William's chair and stares numbly at the floor. Duncan and William exchange glances.)
*William:* (Sitting up and hanging his legs over the edge of the bed) Well?
(Silence from Terry.)
*Duncan:* (Back to the game) See, I told you,

you cannot work your way out of here.

*Terry:* (Slowly looking up at Duncan and then William) Rags, it's all just rags. (Stands up, rips bandanna from his neck, and holds it up, clenched in his fist.) He said all I've done is like filthy rags. My work amounts to nothing. I'll be here until I die! I owe more than when I came.

*Duncan:* Spare me the theatrics. We told you before not to expect so much. In debtor's prison you can't pay for your own debts.

*Terry:* (In anger and frustration, sweeps the checkerboard onto the floor, looks into Duncan's face.) OK, if you have all the answers, then tell me—who can?

*Duncan:* (Standing up face-to-face with Terry, hostile) If I knew the answer to that question, do you think I would be standing here wasting my days in your company? (Gesturing to William) Or his?

*William:* (Gently, to break the tension) Someone able, who cares enough about you to pay your debt, that's who.

*Duncan:* (Glaring at William) And none of us knows anyone like that! (Turns away and begins to pick up the checkers.)

*William:* (To Terry) When Duncan's business

began to fail, he asked his father-in-law for money. His father-in-law is the Duke of Hazards. He lives in the southern part of England and is a very wealthy man. The duke never cared for his daughter's marriage to a commoner, so instead of helping him, he allowed Duncan to be put in prison.

*Duncan:* Poor timing, really. I was about to enter into a partnership with an old Scottish farmer named Ronald. We were intending to open a new shop and name it after him: Ronald McDonald's. We were going to use my fresh bread and his meat to make a special sandwich named the McDuncan or Big Dunc or something like that. But, when my father-in-law would not help me out. . . (His voice trails off.)

*Terry:* (Looking at Duncan) I'm sorry Duncan. You shouldn't be in here.

*William:* None of us should. I would still be in my shop if my landlord had not decided he wanted to put a tavern there. He began to raise the rent until I could no longer pay. By the time I left, he had seized all my instruments. I had nothing with which to pay the back rent, the taxes, or the suppliers for my trade.

*Terry:* (Sitting back down) What're we going to do? We all owe so much. I owe so much. Two years' back rent on the land and a year of food from my brother. It would take a king's ransom to cover my debts. And I don't know anyone with that kind of money.

*Duncan:* Well, I do, and it doesn't make my situation any better.

*Terry:* My wife has written to all our relatives asking them for their help, but they all are in the same situation we are. Except, of course, they've not landed in here.

*William:* (Jumping down from the bed) Wait a minute, chaps, there was a fellow here once who told me a remarkable story. He had heard of a nobleman in the north of England who was known to despise debtor's prisons. The story goes that the nobleman, whom I think was supposed to be a prince, liked to pay off prisoners' debts and thereby secure their release.

*Terry:* (Looking up) I think I've heard that story before. (Thinking) The nobleman was. . .the Duke of Northumberland.

*Duncan:* So what's the rest of the story?

*William:* (Beginning to realize the importance of his story) Apparently a prisoner some years ago wrote a letter to this duke.

*Duncan:* (Intently) And then?

*William:* They say that after a month or so this prisoner packed up and left.

*Terry:* (With new hope) He left alive!

*William:* Pardon me?

*Terry:* You said, "No one leaves alive." This man left alive.

*Duncan:* William! Why have you not remembered this?

*William:* I never really believed it could be true—thought it an old prisoner's wishful tale. Until now. (Shrugging his shoulders) Besides, when I first heard the story, you were ahead of me by 186 games in Checkers. I wanted a chance to catch up.

*Terry:* This is our only hope.

*Duncan:* (With more life and energy than we've seen from Duncan so far) We must contact this gentleman immediately.

*William:* I'll get the phone.

*Duncan and Terry:* The what?

(Fade to black. Blues music up. Fade music out as lights come back up for Scene 3.)

## SCENE 3

(Scene opens with Duncan and William playing Checkers once again. There is a smattering of kings on the board, but the game is even. Duncan and William are somewhat distracted, however, and occasionally glance toward Terry. Terry is lying on the bench but gets up and crosses to the door, looking out the window. He paces nervously and looks uneasy.)

*Narrator:* (Offstage) Duncan, Terry, and William did get a letter out of the prison to the Duke of Northumberland. They explained how their debts were impossible to pay on their own, and they asked for mercy. After that, all they could do was wait.

*Duncan:* (After William moves a checker) Now William, my friend, are you sure that's the move you want to make?

*William:* (Innocently) Why, whatever do you mean?

*Duncan:* It just seems like a rash move, and I'm quite willing to let you make that move again, if you feel for some reason that's not your best choice.

*William:* That's so considerate of you, Duncan.

But I think I'll let my marker stay as it is.

*Duncan:* (He moves a checker, growls.) This game requires no skill whatsoever; it's just a matter of luck!

*William:* (Jumps four checkers.) Ahh. . .got lucky again. King me. . .

*Terry:* (Impatiently) Why has the Duke of Northumberland taken so long to reply? You would think he would at least acknowledge our letter.

*Duncan:* You're sure it was the Duke of Northumberland that was in the story?

*Terry:* (Somewhat irritated) Yes, yes. We've been through this before. (Pause) At least I think it was Northumberland.

*Duncan:* And William, you're certain that he paid the way for this other prisoner to be released?

*William:* (Impatiently) Yes, Duncan. Yes.

*Terry:* (Sitting up) Someone's coming.

(They look at the edge of the stage expectantly, and the guard enters with a rolled-up sheet of paper.)

*Guard:* Terry Coppersmith?

*Terry:* (Nervously) Yes?

*Guard:* I have a message from. . .(looking at the edge of the scroll) the Duke of

Northumberland. (He hands the scroll to Terry.)

(Terry crosses to the front of the table holding the rolled-up message. Duncan and William stand up and come to either side of him. Terry should be right in front of William's chair. Terry holds the paper nervously.)

*Duncan:* (Impatiently) Don't wait all day, man, open it!

*William:* (Gently) Open it, Terry. Read to us what it says.

(Terry carefully unrolls the sheet of paper. He reads the first line silently and then sinks into the chair with a sense of hopelessness.)

*Terry:* (Reading from the letter) "Kind Sirs: On the 31st of May this past year, the Duke of Northumberland died. . ." (He lowers the letter into his lap and looks at the floor.)

*Duncan:* (Disbelieving) He's dead?

*Terry:* (Weakly) He's dead.

*Duncan:* (Frustrated, sits down at the table as he speaks.) Why did I let myself believe that someone else could ever cover my debts? No one cares, and we can no longer help ourselves. It's hopeless.

*William:* (Taking the letter and holding it at arm's length to read it) "Kind Sirs: On the 31st of May this past year, the Duke of Northumberland died. During the duke's life, he secured the release of many a ward from debtor's prisons all across England. When the duke was a boy. . ." (Continues reading to himself, muttering occasionally.)

*Terry:* (Quietly) I'll never see my family again.

*Duncan:* (To himself with disgust) I do not know why I allow myself to get caught up in these irresponsible schemes.

*Terry:* I'll be here the rest of my life. In this room.

*Duncan:* (As he studies the game, all business) William, the game awaits.

*William:* (Growing excited) Listen to this! "But with the death of the Duke of Northumberland comes hope for many in the debtor's prisons of England. For the entire estate and holdings of the duke are being used to secure the release of all prisoners at the Dunsmire Debtor's Prison." (Yells joyfully) His death secures our release. Duncan, Terry, we're free! (Begins playing an imaginary violin and waltzes around the stage, humming, full of joy.)

*Duncan and Terry:* (Blankly) The Dunsmire
   Debtor's Prison?
*William:* (Stopping for a second, pointing to
   the letter) The release is secured for all prisoners at the Dunsmire Debtor's Prison.
   (Comes behind the table and slaps both of
   them on the back.) My friends, we'll be free;
   we ARE free! Our debt is paid! (He looks
   down at the game, pauses, then jumps a
   checker twice.) I believe this game is mine,
   Duncan. (He begins to waltz some more,
   playing the violin.) I shall have a new store
   and make nothing but the finest instruments of exotic woods from around the
   world.
(As Terry stands up to deliver his lines,
   Duncan looks down at the game and quietly begins to reset.)
*Terry:* (Grinning broadly) I'll find a new farm.
   This is a new start, and I'll not waste it.
(William's dancing has brought him to the
   door of the cell; he stops.)
*William:* The door is open. (Looking out)
   Prisoners are running all over out there.
   Duncan, Terry, let us gather our posses-
   sions and go home! (Both he and Terry
   quickly begin to gather up their things.)

*Terry:* (Laughing) I can't wait to see the look
 on my wife's face.

*William:* (Laughs) The look on her face? I
 can't even remember what my wife looks
 like! (William and Terry both laugh again.
 As they turn to head for the door they
 notice Duncan, who is studying the
 checkerboard.)

*Duncan:* (To himself) The key is not to sacrifice too many, too soon. Let the other
 player be aggressive.

*William:* (Gently) Duncan?

*Terry:* The door is open; we're free to go.

*Duncan:* (Firmly, not harshly, not mournfully)
 No one is interested in paying my debt. It's
 my concern. No one cares.

*William:* Ah, but that's no longer true, my
 friend. The death of one man has brought
 freedom for all.

*Terry:* Your debts are paid, Duncan. You're free.
 You have a fresh start. (They move toward
 the door) Come with us. Come! (Terry
 walks offstage.)

*William:* (Hesitates) Duncan, please come.

*Duncan:* I think not. You go.

*William:* Duncan. . .(Pauses, then sadly)
 Good-bye. (Turns and leaves)

*Duncan:* (Sighs as he pushes aside the checkerboard) I think I'll take up Chess.

(Fade to black. Blues music comes up and then
fades out.)

# 6

*The Fruit of the Spirit Is. . .*

# *G*oodness

Look out your window today. What do you see? Is it sunny? Is the wind rustling through the leaves on the trees? Is snow falling gently outside your door? Do robins sing or crickets "crick," or raindrops pitter-patter on your porch? Are children playing down the street? Does the moon loom brightly on a starlit night? Is there anything of beauty wrapped up in your little world?

Of course there is, and each little "present" is yet one more proof of the goodness of God. May this chapter encourage you to notice God's goodness today—and inspire you to imitate His goodness in your life, thoughts, and actions as well.

# The Golden Ax

*The classic fable goes like this. . .*

Once there was a poor but honest woodcutter. Every day he would take his ax of steel, march into the forest and chop enough wood to buy bread for his family.

One day he was chopping down an old oak tree on a river bank when he accidentally knocked the precious ax into the swirling depths of the river.

"What will I do?" wailed the poor man. "I've lost my ax! How will I feed my children?"

Just then a water fairy rose from beneath the surface of the water. "Why are you sad?" she asked. The woodcutter explained how he had clumsily lost his ax.

Feeling pity, the water fairy dove into the river, and came up with an ax of purest silver. "Is this your ax?" she asked.

For a moment the poor woodcutter thought of all the things he could buy with the silver in that ax, then he shook his head and said, "No, my ax is merely made of steel."

The fairy dove under water again, and returned with an ax made of finest gold. "Is this your ax?" she asked as she laid it on the river bank. Again the woodcutter said no—denying a fortune beyond his wildest dreams.

A third time the fairy dove deep into the river, and this time she returned with an ax of steel. "Ahh," said the woodcutter, "that is my ax."

"Take it then," said the fairy, "and because you are a man of good character, you may take the other two axes as a gift from the river." And so the woodcutter had newfound riches to buy all kinds of good things for his family's future.

❧

## GOODNESS IN AMERICA: A STATISTICAL EVALUATION

Consider this:

> More than half of Americans say they will: "drink and drive if I feel that I can handle it" (56 percent); "cheat on my spouse—after all, given the chance he or she will do the same" (53 percent); "do absolutely nothing [at work] one full day in every five" (50 percent).

In spite of the fact that roughly 90 percent of Americans say they "truly believe in God," 84 percent of those same people say that they would willingly "violate the established rules of their religion."

Seventy-four percent of Americans say they will "steal from those who won't really miss it."

Sixty-four percent of Americans say they will "lie when it suits me."

Only 30 percent of Americans would be willing to die for God or their religious beliefs; and 48 percent of Americans say that they have no beliefs they would be willing to die for.

By contrast, for the salary of a professional sports super-star, about one out of every four Americans would do the following: "abandon their church" (25 percent); "abandon their entire family" (25 percent); "become a prostitute for a week or more" (23 percent).

Our young people are not unaffected by the lack of personal character exhibited in our society. According to a recent study by the Josephson Institute of Ethics, one-third of all college students believe that "in today's society, one has to lie or cheat at least occasionally in order to succeed." And, even though 78 percent of high schoolers said cheating on exams is "always wrong," 61 percent admit having cheated within the past year.

There is good news, however. In the area of personal character, faith in God does make a difference. In a landmark, nonreligious study of Americans' private morals, researchers James Patterson and Peter Kim came to this conclusion[23], "Religious people are more moral."

According to Patterson and Kim, religious Americans are:

- better workers;
- more truthful;
- less likely to abuse drugs;
- less likely to commit a petty crime;
- less likely to be swayed by peer pressuren into doing something they know is wrong;
- more committed to their families; and
- more willing to risk their lives for their beliefs.

# A "WHAT'S INSIDE COUNTS" RECIPE

In life—as is often the case in cooking—it's the good stuff on the inside that really counts. Treat yourself to delicious reminders of that truth by baking your own batch of these tasty, good-stuff-on-the-inside cookies!

¾ cup powdered sugar
½ cup butter, softened
1 tablespoon vanilla
1 ½ cups flour
½ teaspoon salt
chocolate kisses, chocolate chips, raisins,
   or other small sweets

Mix powdered sugar, butter, and vanilla. Add in the flour and salt. If mixture is too dry, mix in 1 to 2 tablespoons of milk.

Take about a tablespoon of dough in your hand and mold it around the candy, raisin, or other treat you've chosen. Form a ball with none of the inside goodie showing.

Place cookies about an inch apart on an ungreased cookie sheet. Bake at 350 degrees about 12 minutes. Cookies will not be brown on the tops, but will firm up as they cool.

Makes about 24 cookies.

❦

# A GOOD MAN IS HARD TO FIND[24]

Nate "Tiny" Archibald has always been one of the good guys. His effortless dribble, crisp passes, and soft-touch shooting ability made that much obvious. Whether he was tearing up the basketball courts at the University of Texas-El Paso, or knocking down jump shots on the parquet floor of the Boston Garden, it was clear this guy was good—very good.

In fact, during a fourteen-year career as a professional basketball player, Tiny Archibald was one of the best. From his point guard position, he routinely lit up the boards with both his scoring and deft passing. In 1972–73, he became the only player in NBA history to lead the league in both scoring (averaging 34 points a game) and assists (averaging 11.4 per game) in the same season. As a member of the 1981 Boston Celtics, he helped propel his team to an NBA championship. Six years after he retired, he was easily inducted into the NBA Hall of Fame.

Tiny Archibald showed on the court that he was a good player, but it was off the court where he showed he was also a good person. In his heyday as a basketball legend, Tiny never forgot where he came from: the streets of New York City. During his off-seasons, Tiny always made it a point to return home, running basketball clinics for kids, coaching amateur teams, and even buying equipment for young people.

A few years after his basketball retirement, in 1989, he went home to stay, taking a job as a junior high health and physical education teacher at an inner-city public school in Harlem, New York. While many of his pro basketball Hall of Fame peers have gone on to lucrative careers in business, broadcasting, coaching, and the like, Tiny shunned that big-money kind of work to make a better, longer-lasting investment in people.

"People wonder why I'm back here," Mr. Archibald explained during his ninth year as a professional educator, "but I just love kids. . . . These kids need positive people to take an interest in them."

And so Nate "Tiny" Archibald—NBA legend—has decided to be one of those people.

It's said that a good man is hard to find. But not if you look at the P.S. 175/ I.S. 275 school in Harlem. You'll find him in either the Health or P.E. classroom, sharing a bit of himself with America's future.

✒

## SPEAKING OF GOODNESS. . .

"Goodness is stronger than evil;
   love is stronger than hate;
   light is stronger than darkness;
   life is stronger than death;
   victory is ours through him who loved us."
                    —Bishop Desmond Tutu,
                    as quoted by Mary Batchelor in
                    *The Doubleday Prayer Collection*

"You are never weary, O Lord, of doing us good. Let us never be weary of serving You."
                    —John Wesley,
                    as quoted by Horton Davies in
                    *The Communion of the Saints*

"It is a good thing to do good deeds. It is an even better thing to be a good person."
                    —Anonymous

"I was on the football field at our local high school the other day, where my son was running cross country. As I watched these boys and girls, I was preoccupied with recent problems. I also remembered my cross-country days twenty-five years ago and naturally breathed a prayer of thanksgiving. The prayer was something like, 'Lord, thank you so much that I'm not running cross country any more.'

"Then I sort of loosened up a bit and looked around me. The sky was blue; the leaves were yellow; the air was crisp. I began to enjoy the beautiful day. I forgot my problems and quietly thanked God for the beauty of the world around me. My spirits lifted as I began to appreciate the goodness of God, right there in the middle of the football field."

—John Yates, in a sermon entitled,
"An Attitude of Gratitude"

"Someone has said that the difference between a mere optimist and a Christian optimist is that the former lives by the principle that life is good and the latter by the principle that God is good."

—Robert C. Shannon,
in *1000 Windows*

"Do all the good you can, to all the people you can, in all the ways you can, as often as ever you can, as long as you can."
—Charles Haddon Spurgeon,
as quoted in *Draper's Book of Quotations for the Christian World*

*"Mere acquaintance with a good man is a powerful antidote to evil."*

George MacDonald, in
*The Miracles of Our Lord*

"Books and friends should be few, but good."
—Anonymous

"The Christian is in a different position from other people who are trying to be good. They hope, by being good, to please God if there is one; or—if they think there is not—at least they hope to deserve approval from me. But the Christian thinks any good he does comes from the Christ-Life inside him. He does not think God will love us because we are good, but that God will make us good because He loves us."
—C. S. Lewis in
*Mere Christianity*

"Good will toward all men is a result of the invasion of the supernatural! A state of good intention with 'heartiness and cheerful consent' toward all mankind, if Webster is correct. A state of heart so extraordinary as to be unheard of, except by those who have been hurled out into the place of joyful, utter despair with themselves, where they are finally allowing Jesus Christ to be Himself in them!"

—Eugenia Price, in
*Christianity Today*, volume 1

~

## THE WORD ON GOODNESS

"How great is your goodness [God], which you have stored up for those who fear you, which you bestow in the sight of men on those who take refuge in you."

—Psalm 31:19

"What can I give the LORD for all the good things he has given to me? I will lift up the cup of salvation, and I will pray to the LORD. I will give the LORD what I promised in front of all his people."

—Psalm 116:12–14 NCV

"To this end also we pray for you always, that our God will count you worthy of your calling, and fulfill every desire for goodness and the work of faith with power, so that the name of our Lord Jesus will be glorified in you, and you in Him, according to the grace of our God and the Lord Jesus Christ."

—2 Thessalonians 1:11–12 NASB

*"Great is the LORD*
*and most worthy of praise;*
*his greatness no one can fathom. . . .*
*The LORD is gracious*
*and compassionate,*
*slow to anger and rich in love.*
*The LORD is good to all;*
*he has compassion*
*on all he has made."*

Psalm 145:3, 8–9

"The LORD is my shepherd; I shall not want. He makes me to lie down in green pastures; He leads me beside the still waters. He restores my soul; He leads me in the paths of righteousness for His name's sake.

"Yea, though I walk through the valley of the shadow of death, I will fear no evil; For You are with me; Your rod and Your staff, they comfort me.

"You prepare a table before me in the presence of my enemies; You anoint my head with oil; My cup runs over.

"Surely goodness and mercy shall follow me all the days of my life; And I will dwell in the house of the LORD forever."

—Psalm 23 NKJV

*No exploration of goodness is complete without the story that Jesus once told of a despised, half-Jew, half-Gentile man whose actions revealed the goodness in his heart.*

## THE GOOD SAMARITAN
### (LUKE 10:29–37)

He asked Jesus, "And who is my neighbor?"

In reply Jesus said: "A man was going down

from Jerusalem to Jericho, when he fell into the hands of robbers. They stripped him of his clothes, beat him and went away, leaving him half dead. A priest happened to be going down the same road, and when he saw the man, he passed by on the other side. So too, a Levite, when he came to the place and saw him, passed by on the other side. But a Samaritan, as he traveled, came where the man was; and when he saw him, he took pity on him. He went to him and bandaged his wounds, pouring on oil and wine. Then he put the man on his own donkey, took him to an inn and took care of him. The next day he took out two silver coins and gave them to the innkeeper. 'Look after him,' he said, 'and when I return, I will reimburse you for any extra expense you may have.'

"Which of these three do you think was a neighbor to the man who fell into the hands of robbers?"

The expert in the law replied, "The one who had mercy on him."

Jesus told him, "Go and do likewise."

# A Few Good Words[25]

There's no telling the difference a word of encouragement can make in a person's life. To paraphrase Proverbs 25:11, a few good words, appropriately chosen, are as beautiful as apples of gold in settings of silver. Don't believe it? Maybe Shelly can convince you.

By all accounts, Shelly was just another average student back in her high school days. In fact, she hardly did anything to warrant more than the passing attention of her classmates and teachers. That near-anonymous high school career earned Shelly one memory about her youth. "I got very few compliments," she recalls.

If you were to look at her today (and you probably have), you'd think she wasn't telling the truth about that. You see, she's widely regarded as one of America's most beautiful—and talented—actresses. She's starred in one hit movie after another, performing opposite to Hollywood's most-desired leading men. She's been featured on the cover of America's most prominent magazines, has earned millions with her talent, and has managed to sustain an enduring, successful career as an actress.

Still, in high school, she never dreamed

she'd obtain the kind of success and accolades that would eventually be hers. In fact, she was really just an average kid hungry for a compliment or two.

Which leads us to Shelly's second memory of her teen years: a few good words spoken by an encouraging teacher. Five words in all, not many—but enough.

"I think you have talent," the teacher said. And young Shelly listened, treasuring those words, making them her own.

Today, megastar Michelle Pfeiffer smiles when remembering her teacher's brief affirmation, saying "I never forgot it. It's amazing how something [like that] can alter the direction of your life. I came to feel very confident [about acting] because of that one comment."

A few good words literally changed Michelle Pfeiffer's life. Maybe a few good words from you can do the same thing for someone else too. You'll never know unless you try.

# TOZER ON GOODNESS[26]

*In his classic work,* The Knowledge of the Holy, *theologian A. W. Tozer explains more about what God's goodness really means with these thoughtful insights:*

"The goodness of God is that which disposes Him to be kind, cordial, benevolent, and full of good will toward men. He is tenderhearted and of quick sympathy, and His unfailing attitude toward all moral beings is open, frank, and friendly. By His nature He is inclined to bestow blessedness and He takes holy pleasure in the happiness of His people.

"That God is good is taught or implied on every page of the Bible and must be received as an article of faith as impregnable as the throne of God. It is a foundation stone for all sound thought about God and is necessary to moral sanity. To allow that God could be other than good is to deny the validity of all thought and end in the negation of every moral judgment. If God is not good, then there can be no distinction between kindness and cruelty, and heaven can be hell and hell, heaven.

"The goodness of God is the drive behind

all the blessings He daily bestows upon us. God created us because He felt good in His heart and He redeemed us for the same reason."

‿♪

## GOODNESS KNOWS

Goodness knows that sometimes the greatest thing in the world is a smile from a child,
So Goodness laughs a lot.
Goodness knows it's easier to break a child than to mend one,
So Goodness handles with care.
Goodness knows that everyone deserves a second chance,
And sometimes a third and fourth chance too.
Goodness knows we all need friends in this world,
So Goodness is determined to be friendly.
Goodness knows that only people count,
So Goodness never counts out people.
Goodness knows life is sometimes lonely,
But we are never alone.
And when the sorrows of life are left unexplained, it's still not too much to bear,
For we can trust that Goodness knows.

*Recently Mike was asked to share at our church about his experience with God's goodness during difficult times. Here is what he had to say:*

## GOD IS GOOD.
## ALL THE TIME.

Ever notice that life is often more like a soap opera than a sitcom? In a sitcom, minor crises appear, then are neatly resolved within thirty minutes (including commercials). The happy characters hug at the end, and all is well.

Soap operas, on the other hand, are chock-full of long, drawn out tragedies and emotional extremes. Illnesses last for years, marriages break up with regularity, plane and car wrecks throw characters into comas, evil people scheme and hurt the good folk. And the drama never seems to end until an actor decides to leave the show.

Although our family has more than its share of happy, sitcom times, in the last two years we've also seen some of those soap opera moments crop up in our lives. Like the fall of 1997 when, after seven years of secondary infertility, Amy miraculously got pregnant and then suffered a miscarriage. Or last February, when I held my quietly sobbing son as he was crying himself to sleep because a much-anticipated adoption had just fallen through, and now he knew he would be a big brother to no one. Or last month when a slipped disc in Amy's back became so debilitating she couldn't even sit up to take pain medicine.

But probably the longest running soap opera in our family has been a chronic stomach illness I've had since December of 1996. This illness causes me to feel some level of nausea every day. I call it my own personal "morning sickness." After a routine gallbladder surgery, I started throwing up several times a day and had trouble keeping any food down. I went to a doctor who told me it was all in my head; I should either get over it or learn to live with it. Several weeks—and 25 lost pounds—later, I found a new doctor, but it took him about six months to finally discover what was wrong with me, and more than a year before we arrived at a treatment that's at least 80 percent effective.

Needless to say, persistent nausea has affected every area of my life. I didn't work for three months in 1997, and am now only able to work about thirty hours a week. I've had to drop out of volunteering for youth ministry, cancel projects, withdraw from social events and more. Currently, I'm on a battery of medicines that allows me to function almost normally, and for that I'm grateful. But I am not healed.

Many people have prayed for my healing. The elders of this church have prayed for me twice. Friends and family and many of the kids in our youth group still continue to pray. Two people I trust and respect told me they'd seen visions of God bringing miraculous healing to my body.

But still, I'm not healed. I can't say why God has chosen not to heal me at present, but I can say that even when I'm kneeling in front of the toilet for the umpteenth time, God has also chosen never to leave me.

During the last two years, I've had ample opportunity to examine my faith in Jesus, and I've discovered a few things.

First, I've realized that I do not serve God because of what He does for me, but because of who He is. It doesn't matter if I feel slighted or ignored or wronged by the circumstances God has allowed in my life. What matters is that He is God. Period. End of story. That's why, like Job, I'm trying to become a man who can honestly say, "Though He slay me, yet will I serve Him."

Second, I've learned I must completely trust Jesus for even the smallest details of human accomplishment. I can't take a shower unless Jesus keeps my stomach from churning. I can't work unless Jesus allows me to overcome my daily "morning sickness" and get out of bed. I can't ride to the grocery store unless God protects me from the all-too-frequent carsickness episodes. And, in a way, that's very freeing. My life is not in my control. That means I must truly trust in Him to direct my days. And when I say "God willing, I'll do thus and so," I really mean it now!

Finally, I've seen confirmed the truth that God is good. All the time.

In sickness, He's given me faithful friends who've mightily cared for me and my family. In sorrow, He's given me the comfort of a loving wife and son. In weakness, He's given me strength through His Spirit. In poverty, He's provided miraculous funds. In helplessness, He's given me peace. In hopelessness, He's granted power to persevere.

Like King David in Psalm 27:13 (NIV), I stand before you today to report:

> "I am still confident of this:
> I will see the goodness of the LORD
> in the land of the living."

And, as the very next verse instructs, I intend each day simply to:

> "Wait for the LORD;
> be strong and take heart
> and wait for the LORD."

Thank you.

# 7

*The Fruit of the Spirit Is. . .*

# *F*aithfulness

Over a dozen years ago, we sat choosing songs to be sung at our upcoming wedding ceremony. Although we each tossed out ideas, there was only one that we both knew from the start had to be included: "Great Is Thy Faithfulness."

That old hymn which proclaims "Great is Thy faithfulness, O God my Father. . ." had proven to be true in our separate lives—and continues to be true in our lives together today. If only we were as faithful in everyday life as God is with us! May this chapter encourage us all to strive for that goal.

## Opening Thoughts from Brother Lawrence[27]

"When we are faithful to keep ourselves in His holy presence, it begets in us a holy freedom."

❧

## In Case You Forgot. . .[28]

*In case you forgot, we thought you should know that in many parts of the world, it just isn't safe to live as a faithful Christian. Consider these events that happened as recently as 1998:*

June, 1998. The Saudi Arabian government arrested seven Christians. Their "crimes" were distributing Christian literature and showing the *Jesus* film. In a country that tolerates no religion other than Islam, those are high crimes. One of those arrested was Yolai Aguilar, a woman from the Philippines. Though nine months pregnant, it's believed she was tortured and forced to reveal the names of other Christians in Saudi Arabia. Evidence suggests the other six detainees were also tortured with the same intent.

In this same month, a group of American

Christians visited Chiapas, Mexico, to deliver seven metric tons of food along with medical supplies to refugees in the area. While there, they were attacked by a mob of nationals who threw rocks and sticks at the Americans' bus while shouting "Foreigners get out!" Fortunately, no one was injured.

September, 1998. "All the Christians in the Maldives"—about fifty believers—were reportedly placed in prison. The Maldives, a small island off the coast of India, is overwhelmingly Muslim. Arrested Christians were allegedly detained in small cells and forced to observe Islamic customs such as reading the Koran and reciting Islamic prayers five times a day.

Also in September, 1998, Christians in Laos were reportedly forced to drink boiling water until they revealed the names of other Christians who were giving them Bibles. Those newly exposed Bible-couriers were subsequently detained and also allegedly abused physically.

So, in case you forgot, being a Christian isn't always a painless endeavor for many of your brothers and sisters around the world—and even here at home in America.

Why not take a moment to pray for the faithful who are suffering for Christ today?

# Top Ten Ways to Express Your Faithfulness to God

1. Worship no one other than God.
2. Don't make or worship idols of any kind.
3. Don't misuse God's name.
4. Observe the Sabbath, and keep it holy.
5. Give honor and respect to your parents.
6. Don't murder.
7. Don't commit adultery.
8. Don't steal.
9. Tell the truth.
10. Be satisfied with what you have instead of enviously desiring what someone else has.

*(Paraphrased from Exodus 20:1–17)*

# CHRISTIAN FAITHFULNESS IN AMERICA: A STATISTICAL PICTURE

During 1998, pollster George Barna surveyed over 1,000 U.S. adults to find out their attitudes toward religion. A few of his findings[29]:

> More than eight of every ten Americans (83 percent) rate "religious faith" as something that's very important in their lives.

> Eighty-two percent of those surveyed reported they were "Christian," but only 50 percent said they were "absolutely committed to the Christian faith." And only 39 percent were "born-again Christians."

> Forty-three percent of those surveyed attend church at least once during a given week.

> Nearly two-thirds of those surveyed report they did not read their Bible (other than at church) in the previous week.

Four out of five Americans say they prayed in the previous week, but less than half report participating in other religious activities (such as reading the Bible or attending church) during that same week.

Three out of four adults (77 percent) do not attend Sunday school.

Eighty-two percent of adults do not attend a small group at church.

Only one in four of those surveyed say they've volunteered at church.

Also in 1998, the Yankelovich Partners polled 1,000 American adults, asking whether or not they engaged in religious conversation at work. Turns out[30]:

An overwhelming majority of workers (70 percent) are talking about Jesus and faith in God at the water cooler, in the boardroom, on the auto assembly line, in retail stores, and wherever else they happen to clock in.

Half of Americans (50 percent) talk about religion with their coworkers at least once a month.

Women are twice as likely as men to talk about God at work during any given month. Twenty-nine percent of these ladies broach the topic more than once in a month, whereas only 15 percent of men do the same.

Of those who bring God to work, 85 percent also attend church each week, and 76 percent say they attend church at least once a month.

Surprisingly, however, more than half (54 percent) of those talking about faith also report that they "rarely or never" go to church. That suggests that: 1) Non-Christians are talking about God; and/or 2) Christians are talking about their faith, but not acting on it by joining a community of believers.

# HOLLIS MAYNELL[31]

Lieutenant John Blanchard was determined to be faithful to his country as he served in the U.S. Army during World War II. And at the same time, he longed to be faithful to his heart, a heart which had been stirred just weeks prior while taking a break at a Florida library.

Looking through a book from the stacks, John spotted one that looked interesting. Opening the pages he noticed not what the original author had written, but the gracefully stroked notes softly penciled in the margins. He read a few of those notes, and then a few more. In this anonymous note author, he sensed he'd found a kindred spirit. He was irresistibly drawn to the person who expressed such thoughtful, meaningful prose— even if it was only in the margin of a book.

Flipping to the front page, John found a name to attach to the words he was already beginning to treasure: Miss Hollis Maynell. She had apparently been the previous owner of the book, donating it to the library when she was done with it.

After an exhaustive search that took several weeks, John finally located an address for Miss Maynell in New York City. The day before his unit was to journey overseas for combat in World War II, he wrote a letter to Hollis Maynell, introduced himself, told how he'd come to contact her, and asked if she'd be willing to trade letters with him while he was gone. For the next thirteen months, Miss Maynell did just that, faithfully corresponding with this soldier fighting her country's battles. And with each new letter John received from her, he felt the flush of attraction to this mysterious, yet inwardly beautiful woman.

At one point, John asked for her photograph, but Hollis Maynell declined, telling him that if he really cared for her, it wouldn't matter what she looked like. Finally the time came when John returned home to the United States, and the pen pals set a date for a meeting. On the appointed day, John was to carry a book and wait for her at 7 P.M. at Grand Central Station in New York.

Her letter informed, "You'll recognize me by the red rose I'll be wearing on my lapel."

So, on the appropriate day, at the appropriate time, John Blanchard found himself standing in Grand Central Station, peering intently at passersby for a glimpse of the rose that would identify the woman he had come to love. Here's how he describes what happened next:

*A young woman was coming toward me, her figure long and slim. Her blonde hair lay back in curls from her delicate ears; her eyes were blue as flowers. Her lips and chin had a gentle firmness, and in her pale green suit she was like springtime come alive. I started toward her, entirely forgetting to notice that she was not wearing a rose. As I moved, a small provocative smile curved her lips. "Going my way, sailor?" she murmured.*

*Almost uncontrollably I made one step closer to her, and then I saw Hollis Maynell.*

*She was standing almost directly behind the girl. A woman well past forty, she had graying hair tucked under a worn hat. She was more than plump, her thick-ankled feet thrust into low-heeled shoes. The girl in the green suit was walking quickly away. I felt as though I was split in two, so keen was my desire to follow her, and yet so deep was my longing for the woman whose spirit had truly companioned me and upheld my own.*

*And there she stood. Her pale
plump face was gentle and sensible, her
gray eyes had a warm and kindly twin-
kle. I did not hesitate. My finger
gripped the small worn blue leather copy
of the book that was to identify me to
her. This would not be love, but it
would be something precious, something
perhaps even better than love, a friendship for which I had been and must
ever be grateful.*

*I squared my shoulders and saluted
and held out the book to the woman,
even though while I spoke I felt choked
by the bitterness of my disappointment.
"I'm Lieutenant John Blanchard, and
you must be Miss Maynell. I am so glad
you could meet me; may I take you to
dinner?"*

*The woman's face broadened into a
tolerant smile. "I don't know what this
is about, son," she answered, "but the
young lady in the green suit who just
went by, she begged me to wear this
rose on my coat. And she said if you
were to ask me out to dinner, I should
go and tell you that she is waiting for*

*you in the big restaurant across the street. She said it was some kind of test!"*

❧

## ADVICE ON FAITHFULNESS FROM CHARLES DICKENS TO HIS SON HENRY[32]

As your brothers have gone away one by one, I have written to each of them what I am now going to write you. You know that you have never been hampered with religious forms of restraint, and that with mere unmeaning forms I have no sympathy. But I most strongly and affectionately impress upon you the priceless value of the New Testament, and the study of that book as the one unfailing guide in life. Deeply respecting it, and bowing down before the character of our Saviour, as separated from the vain constructions and inventions of men, you cannot go very wrong, and will always preserve at heart a true spirit of veneration and humility. Similarly, I impress upon you of the habit of saying a Christian prayer every night and morning. These things have stood by me all through my life, and remember that I tried to render the New Testament intelligible to you and lovable by you when you were a mere baby. And so God bless you. Ever your affectionate Father.

✒

## FROM THE MOUTHS OF BABES

Not long ago, the children in our church were learning about baptism. Their teachers carefully explained how this rite of Christianity was endorsed by Jesus, and that Christians have been faithfully performing this rite of faith ever since.

After the lesson, one preschool teacher, Dee Carillo, was tickled to hear her four-year-olds request more information about the topic, though she did have to stifle a chuckle when little Nathan and Jack confused baptism with personal hygiene and asked, "Teacher, how old were you when you were Bathtized?"

# THE WORD ON FAITHFULNESS

"I will sing of the LORD'S great love forever; with my mouth I will make your faithfulness known through all generations. I will declare that your love stands firm forever, that you established your faithfulness in heaven itself. . . . The heavens praise your wonders, O LORD, your faithfulness too, in the assembly of the holy ones. . . .

"O LORD God Almighty, who is like you? You are mighty, O LORD, and your faithfulness surrounds you."

—Psalm 89:1–2, 5, 8

"Let love and faithfulness never leave you; bind them around your neck, write them on the tablet of your heart. Then you will win favor and a good name in the sight of God and man."

—Proverbs 3:3–4

"If we are not faithful, he will still be faithful, because he cannot be false to himself."

—2 Timothy 2:13 NCV

"Be faithful, even to the point of death, and I will give you the crown of life."

—Revelation 2:10

"Unless you are faithful in small matters, you won't be faithful in large ones. If you cheat even a little, you won't be honest with greater responsibilities. And if you are untrustworthy about worldly wealth, who will trust you with the true riches of heaven? And if you are not faithful with other people's money, why should you be trusted with money of your own?"

—Luke 16:10–12 NLT

❧

*The greatest opportunity for faithfulness is found simply in keeping these traditional vows made to a spouse during a wedding ceremony. . .*

## FAITHFUL VOWS

*Minister* (to bride and groom): I now charge you both, as you stand in the presence of God, to remember that true love and faithful observance of your marriage vows are required as the foundation of a successful marriage and the establishment of a happy home. Without these there can be no real marriage and the home which you will endeavor to establish will be a vain effort. Keep the solemn vows you are about to make. Live with tender consideration for each other. Conduct your lives in honesty and in truth. And your marriage will last. Your home will endure. The marriage bond will be a blessing to you, and you will be a blessing to others. This should be remembered as you now declare your desire to be wed. Now, do you (Groom) take this woman to be your wedded wife? And do you solemnly promise, before God and these witnesses, that you will love her, comfort her, honor and keep her in sickness and in health, and that, forsaking all others for her alone, you will perform unto her all the duties that a husband owes his wife, until God, by death, shall separate you?

*Groom*: I do.

*Minister* (to the Bride): Do you (Bride) take this man to be your wedded husband? And do you solemnly promise, before God and these witnesses, that you will love him, comfort him, honor and keep him in sickness and in health, and that, forsaking all others for him alone, you will perform unto him all the duties that a wife owes her husband, until God, by death, shall separate you?

*Bride:* I do.

*Minister:* Since it is your desire to take each other as husband and wife, please join your right hands, face each other, and repeat after me, before God and these witnesses, the marriage vow.

(To the Groom) Repeat after me: "I (Groom's name), take thee (Bride's name) to be my wedded wife, to have and to hold from this day forward, for better or for worse, for richer or for poorer, in sickness and in health, to love and to cherish till death do us part, according to God's holy ordinances and, thereto, I pledge thee my faith.

(To the Bride) Repeat after me: I (Bride's name), take thee to be my wedded husband, to have and to hold from this day forward, for better or for worse, for richer or for poorer, in sickness and in health, to love and to cherish till death do us part, according to God's holy ordinances and, thereto, I pledge thee my faith.

(To all present) Now, those whom God has
joined together, let no man put asunder.

❧

## FAITHFUL VOWS,
## PART 2

Remembering her first date with a specific man
Sylvia shares, "He confessed that he was married, but that his wife was in a nursing home
permanently, having suffered a severe stroke
years ago. *Nice try*, I thought. *I happen to know
the lady; she's in my book club.*"[33]

We wryly laugh at Sylvia's experience, thinking what a cad this man must be to lie so
brazenly. Yet would we have had different feelings for him if his story were true? Would we
have justified his seeking a date with a young
woman if his wife were, in reality, wasting away
in a nursing home?

Those wedding vows, the ones that go, "In
sickness and in health," or the part that says,
"till death do us part." How seriously do people
take these? Surely there are many who, like
Sylvia's date, think nothing of the vows they
once made. When times get tough, it's time to

move on. But a vow is a vow, and the faithful do not make vows lightly—or forget them quickly.

Morris Forman is such a man. He easily remembers meeting his wife Eve over fifty years ago. Back in the days when there were rules to courting, Eve was bold enough to knock on the door of Morris's New York home and tell him he'd been "recommended" to her by her cousin.

"A woman calling on a man, boy, that never happened in those days," Morris recalls. "I was so lucky."

Morris married bold young Eve and they've been married fifty years now. Morris loves his wife just as much, even after all these years. Even after all the changes that have occurred. And what sad changes they are.

Morris and Eve were unable to have children, so Eve became "Aunt Eve" to all the neighborhood kids. Now Eve is certain a stuffed doll is the child she never had and clings to it constantly.

Eve was once a bookkeeper, with a mind so bright she was able to quickly multiply three-digit numbers in her head. That same mind now can't tell her fingers how to use a spoon.

The long walks they once enjoyed are now taken down the halls of a nursing home. You've probably guessed. Eve has Alzheimer's. So while Morris recalls the Eve that once was, the marriage that once was, the love that once was, Eve remembers nothing. This cruel disease has stolen her memories.

Yet Morris is faithful. He visits Eve every day. He holds her hand. He talks to her quietly. He holds a weekly sing-along for Eve and the other residents. He holds his wife close and tells her he loves her, because he still does. As Morris puts it, "Just because someone has a disease doesn't mean the love is gone."[34]

∿

*Ever wonder what would happen if we sports fans applied our attitudes about church faithfulness to our favorite teams? It might look something like this treatise from an anonymous fan:*

## WHY I'VE STOPPED SUPPORTING MY TEAM
by an Ex-Sports Fan

1.  Whenever I go to a game, they ask for money.

2. The other fans don't care about me.
3. The seats are too hard.
4. Coach never visits me.
5. The referee makes calls I don't agree with.
6. Some of the games go into overtime and make me late for dinner.
7. The band plays songs I don't know.
8. I have other things to do at game time.
9. My parents took me to too many games when I was growing up.
10. I know more than the coaches anyway.
11. I can be just as good a fan at the lake.
12. I won't take my kids to a game either. They must choose for themselves which teams to follow.

## THANK GOD FOR FAITHFUL PASTORS![35]

Sure, it looks like an easy job. A pastor only works Sundays, right? And spends the rest of the week golfing. And gets paid to read the Bible. And is widely respected, well loved, and living happily ever after with the church family, right?

Don't count on it. Although a pastor's life can include those elements, a recent study by *Leadership* magazine revealed pastors often serve faithfully in a thankless job.

Consider:

On average, a pastor labors about fifty-five hours per week on the job.

A pastor typically works more evenings and weekends than most other American professionals do.

Pastors invest roughly eleven hours a week in preparation for a Sunday morning sermon that usually only lasts thirty to forty-five minutes—and is mostly forgotten within an hour after church ends.

Over half of America's pastors have never had any time management training, but are expected to juggle a dizzying array of administrative and pastoral duties without any complications whatsoever.

Nearly half of our pastors say they're working too hard—yet nine out of ten pastors still say they find satisfaction in the work they do.

Why not take a moment today to thank God—and your pastor—for pastors.

⌇

*Recently Mike had the opportunity to chat with renowned pastor and author Max Lucado. During their conversation, Max shared a bit about how he had learned the importance of being faithful in prayer while stationed as a missionary in Brazil. Here's what Max had to say:*

## Max Lucado on Becoming Faithful in Prayer[36]

*Max L.:* The prayer life for me really came to life when I was a missionary in Brazil. Our church was a missionary church; it was a small, struggling, storefront congregation. And a man came to be a part of our church who became a Christian through a Pentecostal movement in Brazil.

He was a wonderful Christian man who had a drug problem. And he came to Rio de Janeiro, Brazil, right out of a drug rehab center. And this Pentecostal drug rehab center turned that man into a prayer warrior. This is incredible, Mike, but it's the truth. He was required in that rehab center to spend three hours each day on his knees—from six to seven in the morning, from twelve to one at lunch, and then from six to seven in the evening.

I remember he told me, "Whether we prayed or not was up to us, but we had to be on our knees." And he came to our church—I think the Lord sent him our way—and his first question to us was "Why don't you pray?" And we said, "Well, we pray. I mean. . .you know." So he said, "Why don't you pray?" And so I would meet him every afternoon for an hour of prayer in our little church building.

*Mike N.:* Can you share his name?

*Max L.:* Yeah, I can. I honestly don't remember his last name. It's been over twelve years since I've seen him! But his first name was Abel. Wonderful, nice-looking, young man. Fiery, fiery man. Real committed to Christ.

And so the two of us would get down on our knees in that little church building, get on the concrete floor, and he would rock back and forth on his knees and he would pray. He'd say, "Oh, Lord, equip the church. Lord, equip the church. Equip the church." He'd just say it over and over again. He was just so passionate in his prayers. And with time, that became contagious to me. I think I learned what James means when he says, "The earnest prayers of a faithful man availeth much." For I saw in him earnest prayers.

I would love to have a more earnest prayer life! Mike, in my life, prayer is the single most difficult discipline. I love God and there's something in me that would rather do things for God than talk to God. I'm not by nature a mystical, devotional person. I like to do things. And so it's a challenge for me to have a faithful prayer life, but I know God loves me and He's not mad at me. He just wishes I would slow down and turn things over to Him. And that's what I think you achieve through prayer.

❧

# PARTING THOUGHTS FROM CHARLES W. COLSON[37]

"God calls me to be faithful, not successful. The end result is in His hands, not mine."

# 8

*The Fruit of the Spirit Is. . .*

# Gentleness

It's true that we live in a harsh world, but it's also true that gentleness invades that harshness with its own kind of beauty. We see it in the way a mother cradles a newborn baby, in the eyes of a father roughhousing with a preschooler, in the silence of a setting sun, in the affectionate caress of a lifetime lover and friend, in the peace that settles during an anxious prayer, and in a thousand ways more.

Yes, gentleness is invading your world today. The only question is whether or not you've joined the revolution.

# GENTLE JESUS, MEEK AND MILD
by Charles Wesley

Gentle Jesus, meek and mild,
Look upon a little child;
Pity my simplicity,
Suffer me to come to Thee.

Lamb of God, I look to Thee;
Thou shalt my example be:
Thou art gentle, meek and mild;
Thou wast once a little child.

Fain I would be as Thou art;
Give me Thine obedient heart:
Thou art pitiful and kind;
Let me have Thy loving mind.

Loving Jesus, gentle Lamb,
In Thy gracious hands I am;
Make me, Saviour, what Thou art,
Live Thyself within my heart.

*In his powerful book,* Choosing to Live the Blessing, *John Trent shares memories of the gentle touch of his mother's hands—and how that gentleness shaped who he is today. Listen as he shares it now with you. . .*

## PICTURES OF MY MOTHER
### by John Trent

Like Robert Cormier, when I think of my childhood, my thoughts stumble upon a thousand pictures of my mother's hands. But for different reasons.

She couldn't untie knotted shoestrings, button winter coats, iron shirts, or straighten ties. Simple things, but she couldn't do them. From my earliest memory, my mother's hands were bent and twisted with rheumatoid arthritis. The world wouldn't think them beautiful, but they were beautiful to me and to my brothers. They became, over the years, a symbol of her love for us.

Because of the pain in those twisted joints, my mother could not grab your hand. She never took your hand and shook it. When she took it, she touched it gently, squeezing just a part of it. Holding on to you softly. Then releasing you from her touch.

That's how she held on to each of us boys. Tenderly. Softly. With great affection and warmth. And yet loosely.

I remember when [my twin brother] Jeff and I turned ten, she dressed us up in our finest sports coats and clip-on ties. Her hands weren't strong enough to tie a real knot, and there was no man around the house to do it. She took us to a fancy restaurant, and at dinner she made sure we knew that we were now "young men" and were expected to act as such. After dinner, she gave us each a dollar and told us, to our amazement, that we were to leave the tip. It was a rite-of-passage for us, for from that day on we were expected to take more and more responsibility. My mother never paid another bill or left another tip when we were with her. She would slide us the money under the table, and we would assume that duty. We were learning, through her soft hands and gentle proddings, to become gentlemen. We were beginning to grow up. And she was beginning to let go.

Mom consistently loved us passionately and yet held on to us loosely in love. The day Jeff and I turned sixteen she drove us to get our driver's licenses. Thirty minutes later she let us drive our old Volkswagen twelve hundred miles from Phoenix to Indianapolis to see our uncle. She wanted to go with us, but her hands and knees were too painful to sit scrunched in a small car for that long. Every time I look back, I marvel at the loose hold she had on our lives.

She held everything loosely. Cups. Silverware. Pencils. She even held the days loosely, never knowing whether it would be a good day or a bad one, taking what came and taking it with grace. If her gentle touch helped us grow up, it also provided a strong incentive to do what was right. Because her hands hurt so much, my mother was never able to spank us, but beneath her tender ways there was an underlying firmness. Worse than a spanking was when she would place her hand on ours, always gently, and speak to us, always gently, of her concern about our behavior. When she looked up at you and held your hand, you might as well have been in the grip of a lumberjack. You couldn't pull away. It would hurt her hands if you did. So you sat there. And you listened. And little by little, the warmth of her heart melted yours.

I have pictures in my mind of her typing, bending down to the keyboard, leaning a little to the right and typing at an angle. It's the way most people with rheumatoid arthritis have to type, if they can type at all. She would sit at the typewriter until the wee hours of the morning typing reports for us. I never thought much about those pictures then. Now I can't get them out of my mind. . .or my heart. . .

Four years after my dad left the hospice, my mom entered it. Her room was just three doors down from his. There she spent the last four months of her life.

This day I was pacing the hall outside that room, a bright orange form in my hand, trying to put off the inevitable.

We had talked about it a dozen times over the years and especially in the months leading up to this day. Yesterday I had gone over the whole thing again with Mom's primary care physician and the head nurse. And now I was the one who had to do it.

I was the one who had to walk into my mother's room, set that bright orange form in front of her, and have her sign it. It was the form reflecting her wish that there be no medical heroics in the last hours of her life.

It was the most difficult moment of my life.

Here sat my mother, my sweet, precious mother. Those bright piercing eyes. Her thinning snow-white hair. Her hands so warm and soft. We sat and held hands and talked. She was brave and courageous as ever.

I was a mess.

I cried at the thought of losing someone

who had loved me and blessed me since the day I was born. A thousand memories washed over me. Of walks and hugs, of breakfasts at the old kitchen table, and of camping trips in our beat-up old trailer. The days watching the Dodgers in spring training. The midnight runs for my can collection. Late-night crackers. I couldn't keep the tears from my eyes as I thought of losing her listening ear, her gentle love, her precious life.

It was the worst day of my life. How many more days would we have her? Two, three. A week?

Two weeks later, [my brother] Joe and I were keeping vigil in her room. I was sitting in the chair, taking the first shift. He was sleeping in the bed next to her. At 2:20 in the morning, her breathing grew shallow and irregular.

By now she had become so dehydrated she was unable to speak. But she didn't need to. She had said "I love you" hundreds of times with words and thousands of times with the pictures she left behind. No words needed to be spoken. No words needed to be heard.

As her breathing slowed, we moved our chairs next to her, one boy on each side, holding her hands. Hands that brushed away our tears and patted us gently when we had done well in sports or in school. Hands that put back so carefully the pieces of a broken heart. We nestled next to her just like when we were kids, when we got scared, or lonely, or just wanted to know that everything would be all right.

Only this time everything wouldn't be all right. This time she wouldn't be able to hug away the hurt.

Neither would we.

She breathed one last shallow breath. Neither Joe nor I moved. For several minutes we sat by her side, still and silent. Maybe if no one spoke, if no one stood up, if no one called the nurse, maybe we could somehow postpone the loss. Neither of us wanted to admit we had just lost our mother. . .and that we were now orphans.

I touched her hands for the last time. Those incredibly soft and tender hands.

I pray the first hands I see in heaven are the nail-scarred hands of my Savior.

And that the next ones I see are my mommy's.

Now straightened and strong.

But still soft and caring and lovely as I remembered them that day. . .and as I will remember them always.

# The Word on Gentleness

"Are there those among you who are truly wise and understanding? Then they should show it by living right and doing good things with a gentleness that comes from wisdom."

—James 3:13 NCV

*"Let your gentleness be
evident to all."*

Philippians 4:5

"I, therefore, the prisoner of the Lord, beseech you to walk worthy of the calling with which you were called, with all lowliness and gentleness, with longsuffering, bearing with one another in love."

—Ephesians 4:1–2 NKJV

"A gentle answer turns away wrath, but a harsh word stirs up anger."

—Proverbs 15:1

"But in your hearts set apart Christ as Lord. Always be prepared to give an answer to everyone who asks you to give the reason for the hope that you have. But do this with gentleness and respect, keeping a clear conscience, so that those who speak maliciously against your good behavior in Christ may be ashamed of their slander."

—1 Peter 3:15–16

## THE WIND AND THE SUN
### A Fable by Aesop

Once upon a time when everything could talk, the Wind and the Sun fell into an argument as to which was the stronger. Finally, they decided to put the matter to a test: they would see which one could make a certain man, who was walking along the road, throw off his cape.

The Wind tried first. He blew and he blew and he blew. The harder and colder he blew, the tighter the traveler wrapped his cape about him. The Wind finally gave up and told the Sun to try.

The Sun began to smile and as it grew warmer and warmer, the traveler was comfortable once more. But the Sun shone brighter and brighter until the man grew so hot, the sweat poured out on his face. He became weary, and seating himself on a stone, he quickly threw his cape to the ground.

You see, gentleness had accomplished what force could not.

<br>

## SPEAKING OF GENTLENESS. . .

"In our rough-and-rugged individualism, we think of gentleness as weakness, being soft, and virtually spineless. Not so! . . . Gentleness includes such enviable qualities as having strength under control, being calm and peaceful when surrounded by a heated atmosphere, emitting a soothing effect on those who may be angry or otherwise beside themselves, and possessing tact and gracious courtesy that causes others to retain their self-esteem and dignity. . . . Instead of losing, the gentle gain. Instead of being ripped off and taken advantage of, they come out ahead!"

—Charles R. Swindoll,
as quoted in *Draper's Book
of Quotations for the
Christian World*

"Although the world tells us to be assertive, the Word tells us to be gentle."

—Florence Littauer, in
*The Best of Florence Littauer*

"I've learned that a hug from my husband sends his strength into my body."

—39-year-old woman,
as quoted in *The Complete Live
and Learn and Pass It On*

*"Lord, make my words soft
and gentle today. . . .
I may have to eat them tomorrow!"*

Anonymous prayer

"Gentleness and consideration are qualities ascribed to Jesus himself, even though He is the all-powerful King. . . . Strikingly, [gentleness] is one of the traits required in spiritual leaders and is a mark of spiritual maturity and of responsiveness to God's Spirit. It is also the way set out in the New Testament for believers to respond to opposition."

—Lawrence O. Richards, in
*Expository Dictionary of Bible Words*

"Advice is like snow; the softer it falls, the longer it dwells upon and the deeper it sinks into the mind."

> —Samuel Taylor Coleridge,
> as quoted in *Christian Reader*,
> Vol. 33, number 1

"It's easier to get close to someone when there are no hard edges."

> —Roman the Teddy Bear,
> as quoted in Susan E. Schwartz's
> *Teddy Bear Philosophy*

"God strikes with his finger, and not with all his arm."

> —George Herbert,
> in *Jacula Prudentum*

"Gentleness is love's conduct."

> —Paul Nadon,
> in an Internet posting

"Many of us believe gentleness is something beyond our reach. Of course, that is simply not true. We can become gentle people, because God is gentle."

> —James A. Chase,
> in the Internet sermon,
> "A Recipe for Right Relationships, Part 8"

# No Match for Third Grade?

By all rights, Darlene Hanneman is no match for a classroom full of rowdy third-graders. Third-graders are loud and excitable. Darlene is quiet and calm. Third-graders are easily distracted by flashy events happening outside—like another class breaking early for recess. Darlene is focused and deliberate. Third-graders need a teacher with a foghorn-like voice to cut through the chatter with the day's homework assignments. Darlene speaks in a mild, pleasant tone, more like a hummingbird than a foghorn.

In short, the gentle woman should be hopelessly outgunned when faced with the task of teaching eight- and nine-year-olds important subjects like reading, writing, and arithmetic. And yet, she's one of the best.

Instead of yelling for kids to be quiet, she silences with a gaze or a gentle touch on a child's shoulder. Instead of being feared, she's respected. Instead of loudly cheering a child's accomplishment, she warms him or her with a sincere smile.

When our son entered Darlene's class, we wondered if Tony and his energetic classmates would soon overwhelm her. Then she came to visit Tony in our home. We noticed his immediate responsiveness to her gentle style. As she sat on our couch, she pleasantly invited him to sit next to her, giving him her full attention when he spoke and reassuring his contributions to the conversation with a light touch on the knee. She clearly explained her expectations regarding Tony's classroom conduct, but without resorting to the "fire-and-brimstone" style speech that usually accompanies such talk.

Later, we observed her deftly directing two dozen kids in a series of dramatic readings for parents. As we watched our son happily—and carefully—reading his part as "Toad" in a *Frog and Toad* story, we realized he was performing for her as much as he was for us. Her gentle and caring spirit had won him over, and it showed.

Yes, it might look like the soft-spoken and grandmotherly demeanor of Darlene Hanneman is no match for third-graders, but appearances can be deceiving. In fact, this wonderful teacher is the perfect match for this classroom, and we think parents can learn a lot from her as well.

# A Prayer of Mary Batchelor[38]

Lord Jesus, give me your gentleness.

Make me sensitive to others' needs, quick to discern even when no words are spoken.

Help me never to rush in with thoughtless words, nor to brush others aside with sweeping assertions.

Help me never to quench another's hopes nor deepen another's sorrow, but to pour your peace and balm, your comfort and love on all those I meet today. Amen.

*In 1 Kings chapter 19, the Bible records a surprisingly gentle encounter Elijah the prophet had with God. We'd like to retell it for you here in our own words. . .*

## God in a Whisper

Elijah couldn't help but smile and feel proud of himself. He—well, God really—had just defeated hundreds of the false prophets Queen Jezebel had set up to lead the people of Israel in worshiping bloody idols of evil. The contest had been fantastic! In the end, God had swooped down with a blaze of fire and defeated once and for all the terrible power of Jezebel's false religion.

Or so it seemed.

As Elijah sat breathing the sweet breath of victory, he saw a messenger approaching. Moments later, the runner delivered this news: "King Ahab has told his wife Queen Jezebel about everything that happened today, and about how all her prophets have been killed. The Queen sends this message to you, Elijah: 'May the gods deal with me, be it ever so severely, if by this time tomorrow I do not make your life like that of one of them.'"

Sudden fear seized Elijah's heart. That madwoman was going to kill him! Elijah didn't waste any time. Immediately, he gathered his few things and ran for his life! He ran until he could run no more, and found himself a day's journey into the desert. There, he fell down under the branches of a broom tree and prayed.

"Where are you now, Lord? Have you gone away and taken your power with you? Why not end it right now, Lord? Why not kill me where I sit instead of making me wait for Jezebel's men to come and slit my throat? Oh, God, where have you gone and why did you leave me?"

Elijah collapsed in a heap under the tree and wept. Then he sat up with a start—something was poking him! Through slitted eyes Elijah was stunned to see an angel standing beside him, standing as if he'd been there all the time.

"Get up and eat," the angel said simply. And he produced bread and water. Elijah ate, drank, and lay back down. Not long after, the angel appeared again, this time saying "Get up and eat, for the journey is too much for you." Elijah obeyed.

Strengthened by this food from heaven, Elijah traveled forty days and nights across the desert until he reached Mount Horeb, the mountain of God. He slept that night in a cave at the base of the mountain.

Next morning, he heard the voice of God speaking to him. "What are you doing here, Elijah?"

The prophet replied, "I have been very zealous for the LORD God Almighty. The Israelites have rejected your covenant, broken down your altars, and put your prophets to death with the sword. I am the only one left, and now they are trying to kill me too."

God commanded, "Go out and stand on the mountain in the presence of the Lord, for the Lord is about to pass by."

Almost before Elijah could reach the entrance to the cave, he felt the wind—a rushing, mighty wind that tore through the landscape and left a waste of desolation behind it. Tree limbs cracked and broke in the face of the wind. Boulders rolled and shattered. Stinging dirt and dust blinded Elijah's eyes. But the Lord did not come.

Finally, the wind died down, and following closely on its heels Elijah felt the ground begin to tremble. In seconds a mighty earthquake cracked the ground, a yawning, terrible groan that surely announced the arrival of the Lord. . . But still, the Lord did not come.

After the earthquake came a monstrous fire that devoured everything it happened to touch. Elijah stood in fear, terrified he would soon be swallowed up in the flames of God. Almost as abruptly as it had come, the fire disappeared, leaving behind the sooty rubble of its destruction.

But still, in spite of the awesome power of the fire, the Lord had not come.

After the fire, silence filled the mountain. The world was still, nothing moving or turning. Elijah sat like a stone, unsure of whether or not he was even breathing.

Then he heard it. A gentle whisper caressed the battered ground, toying with his hearing in delightful tones. The whisper came again, and Elijah couldn't help but smile, sensing the Presence that accompanied the voice.

God had finally come, not in earthshaking power, but in the gentle, fragrant voice of a Friend.

❦

*In his enchanting children's novel,* The Lion, the Witch and the Wardrobe, *C. S. Lewis relates a beautiful example of gentleness bound in strength. In this scene, the great Lion, Aslan (a Christ-figure in the book), has just risen from the dead and greeted two of the children who love him, Susan and Lucy Pevensie, in front of the Stone Table where he had previously been executed. . .*

## ASLAN'S ROMP[39]

"Oh, children," said the Lion, "I feel my strength coming back to me. Oh, children, catch me if you can!" He stood for a second, his eyes very bright, his limbs quivering, lashing himself with his tail.

Then he made a leap high over their heads and landed on the other side of the Table. Laughing, though she didn't know why, Lucy scrambled over it to reach him. Aslan leaped again. A mad chase began. Round and round the hilltop he led them, now hopelessly out of their reach, now letting them almost catch his tail, now diving between them, now tossing them in the air with his huge and beautifully velveted paws and catching them again, and now stopping unexpectedly so that all three of them rolled over together in a happy laughing heap of fur and arms and legs. It was such a romp as no one has ever had except in Narnia; and whether it was more like playing with a thunderstorm or playing with a kitten Lucy could never make up her mind. And the funny thing was that when all three finally lay together panting in the sun the girls no longer felt in the least tired or hungry or thirsty.

## A CLOSING PRAYER[40]

Lord of the gentle hands, may mine be gentle too.

# 9

*The Fruit of the Spirit Is. . .*

# Self-Control

Wouldn't it be great if Adam and Eve had never given in to temptation? If they'd resisted the desire to taste the forbidden fruit in the Garden of Eden? If they'd exhibited enough self-control to save us all from that original sin?

But, sadly, they did give in to the serpent's tempting, and humanity has been paying the price ever since. Perhaps it's time we learn from their failure, and ask God to help us practice self-control, to resist temptation, and to let our lives glorify Him. As we understand it, it's never too late to start obeying God.

# Small Start, Big Finish

It all started with a cotton ball. That's it, really.

Well, there were also two doctors involved. Dr. Mohan Korgaonkar was the surgeon, and Dr. Kwok Wei Chan was assisting as the anesthesiologist. The patient shall remain nameless.

So there they were, Dr. Korgaonkar, Dr. Chan, our long-suffering patient (sleeping, thank goodness), and the cotton ball.

The date was October 24, 1991, and all was going as planned. An operation was scheduled and underway in a Worcester, Massachusetts, hospital. Dutifully doing his job, Dr. Chan administered the anesthesia, sending our patient into a deep slumber. With a confidence that comes from years of experience, Dr. Korgaonkar deftly began the procedure. All was going well.

Except, it seems, for our two physicians. No one knows for sure what words passed between them, but the intent was clear. These men didn't like each other.

Silently the minutes ticked by, and with each passing moment the tension in the operating room grew thicker. And thicker.

Perhaps Dr. Chan was a "backseat surgeon," offering unwanted advice about the surgeon's technique. Perhaps Dr. Korgaonkar told a belittling joke about anesthesiologists in general, or about Dr. Chan in particular. Perhaps one was having a bad hair day and the other noticed. Or, most likely, perhaps the two physicians were feeling a bit cranky, stressed, and tired.

Whatever the reason, at one point during the operation, something about Dr. Chan irked the surgeon. Almost without thinking, Dr. Korgaonkar flicked a cotton ball disdainfully at the anesthesiologist. Apparently, the surgeon was a good aim, because Dr. Chan retaliated.

Next came pushing and shouting. Then an all-out brawl between the two men of medicine. Fists flying and medical goals forgotten, the doctors eventually escalated into a wrestling-punching-jabbing-name-calling bout on the operating room floor. Both doctors had completely lost any semblance of self-control, their only aim to satisfy their rage.

And our patient? Slept through it all.

Finally the two men tired a bit, regained their composure, got up, and finished the operation. Not long after, both were fined $10,000 by the state Board of Registration in Medicine, and ordered to submit to joint psychotherapy for their aggressive tendencies.

And to think, it all started with a cotton ball.[41]

It only took a little cotton ball to send two respected doctors over the edge and into fisticuffs. And for their little indulgence, they succeeded in cheapening their reputation and the reputation of doctors in general. Truly, the $10,000 fine was the smallest fee they paid!

*We would be wise to take a lesson from these poor examples of self-control. Hey, if a teeny little cotton ball can tear up a whole operating room, there's no telling what might happen if we don't!*

❧

## A DESERT PARABLE[42]

The story goes something like this:

Two travelers embarked on a dangerous journey across the desert. At first, all seemed to be going well. There was plenty of water, and the company was pleasant. But midway through the journey, one traveler noticed the terrain had suddenly become a vast, unrecognizable plain. Slowly their water supplies dwindled. They continued on, fear beginning to gnaw at their hearts. Finally, their fear became a reality.

They were lost and alone in the merciless, fiery desert.

Throats drying, lips parching, and now with water scarce, they wandered on hoping to find a way out. One day passed, then two. Finally, on the fifth day, when they were weak and dying of thirst, a miracle appeared. A stranger came into view, a man with camels and life-giving water!

The two travelers collapsed in a heap and prayed the stranger would see them—and he did. Moments later he stood before them, taking in the situation.

"Help me! Help me!" croaked the first traveler. "Need water! Must have water! Give me water! Water!"

The second traveler said nothing.

The first traveler began clawing at the stranger, all the while pleading and begging for water. Still, the second man said nothing, waiting. Intrigued, the stranger broke free from the first traveler and knelt down beside the second.

"Are you thirsty?" the stranger inquired.

"Yes. Very," he replied.

"Then why do you not cry out for water like your friend here?"

"The water belongs to you," said the second

traveler. "If you choose to share it, I won't have to ask."

Impressed by this traveler's self-restraint even in harsh circumstances, the stranger unstoppered his flask and poured the life-giving liquid down the thirsty man's throat. Only after the second traveler had drunk his fill did the first get his share.

Self-control had won what wailing demands had not.

◆

## DISCIPLINE YOURSELF (NO ONE ELSE WILL)
### by Bruce & Stan

Humans are funny beings. It used to be that many of us wanted every material thing we could get our hands on, and we wanted whatever it was to be bigger, better, or faster. Then we discovered that *outward* material things don't make us happy. So over the last few years we've turned *inward*. We've decided that it's what's inside that counts. Consequently, many of us have embarked on an inward journey, seeking to simplify our lifestyles while increasing our joy.

At least that's the goal, because that's what the simplicity gurus are telling us in books like *Simple Abundance* and *Living the Simple Life*.

The idea of simplifying your life is a good one. . . . The problem is that we are attacking the goal with the same unbridled zest we used to collect all that stuff in the first place. Like a crazy pendulum, we swing from one extreme to the other with gusto, somehow feeling empty at both places.

So how do you find the satisfaction you've been looking for? The key is balance, consistency, and perseverance, all of which come from one thing and one thing only: *discipline.*

Here's our dilemma. We want it all, and we want it now, whether it's an abundance of possessions or an abundance of simplicity. But nothing worthwhile comes quickly, and nothing worthwhile comes without discipline. Over life's long haul, discipline works in every dimension of your life: financial, physical, mental, and spiritual. If you've ever tried to get rich quick, tried to lose weight by taking a pill, tried to get knowledge by cramming at the last minute, or attempted to get close to God by asking for a miracle, you know what we're talking about.

It's easy to get caught in the trap of quick

results when you focus on the results rather than the journey. The truth is, the joy is in the journey, in the daily discipline of growing in the details of your mind, body, and spirit. The only way to bring abundance to your life—the kind of abundance that gives you joy—is to bring discipline into your life. . .

- Discipline begins with small things done daily.
- The secret behind most success stories? Discipline.
- Every morning you choose your attitude for the day.
- The first step on the path to commitment is making up your mind.
- You can plan to succeed or you can plan to fail. The choice is yours.
- Motivation increases when we assume large responsibilities with a short deadline.
- Develop a cause for your life. Whatever it is, dedicate yourself to it daily.
- Don't be good at making excuses.
- Discipline is at the heart of discipleship.
- Before diving into anything, step back and view the big picture.

- Acquire good habits; abandon bad habits.
- Move from involvement to commitment.
- Use your free time productively.
- Your dreams won't come true if you allow them to languish.
- Your dreams won't come true if you're sleeping.
- If you want to achieve excellence, begin with discipline.
- Worthwhile activities may be tough in the short-term but rewarding in the long-term.
- People will be more impressed by what you finish than by what you start.
- Motivation can fade. Habits prevail.

<br>

❧

*Unfortunately, American society isn't known for its self-control, and so we often reap the dismal rewards of our own bad habits. . .*

## AMERICA'S BAD HABITS[43]

There are approximately sixty-one million cigarette smokers in the United States today, or roughly 29 percent of the U.S. population aged twelve and older. Those smokers incur a cost of an estimated $60 billion a year in smoking-related health care (not counting lost productivity for missing work on account of a smoking-related illness). Also, an estimated 400,000 deaths per year are attributed to smoking cigarettes.

Smokers tend to drink twice as much alcohol as non-smokers, and a smoker's risk of drinking too heavily is ten to fourteen times higher than that of a non-smoker. Additionally, smokers are over four times more likely to abuse illicit drugs than non-smokers.

Americans spend over $100 billion each year on alcohol consumption. Alcohol is involved in 44 percent of the nation's annual traffic-accident fatalities, a number that's roughly equal to 17,600 people each year. One of alcohol's many negative side effects, liver cirrhosis, is the eleventh leading cause of death among Americans. Additionally, roughly one out of every three deaths by drowning is alcohol-related.

With nearly sixty-nine million Americans over age twelve using it, marijuana is the most frequently used illegal drug in the U.S.A. Marijuana hinders a person's short-term memory, warps perceptions, and slows reaction time. With that in mind, it's no surprise to discover that one study revealed that roughly one-third of hospital trauma patients are admitted due to marijuana-related accidents. Additionally, the likelihood of using cocaine has been estimated to be more than 104 times greater for those who have tried marijuana than for those who have never tried it.

Roughly twenty-two million Americans have used cocaine, one of the most addictive drugs of abuse. One out of every ten people who begin using cocaine "recreationally" will go on to serious, heavy abuse of this drug. As recently as 1995, the number of cocaine-related hospital emergencies during a given year was over 140,000 incidents, or roughly one-fourth of all drug-related emergency room treatments.

We could go on, but we're betting you get the picture. Individual Americans' inability to exercise self-control has resulted in deadly habits for America as a whole. Are you part of these statistics? Perhaps you can change them for the better, starting right now.

# THE FLIES AND THE HONEY POT[44]
## by Aesop

A jar of honey chanced to spill
Its contents on the windowsill
In many a viscous pool and rill.

The flies, attracted by the sweet,
Began so greedily to eat,
They smeared their fragile wings and feet.

With many a twitch and pull in vain
They gasped to get away again,
And died in aromatic pain.

Moral:
O foolish creatures that destroy
Themselves for transitory joy.

# A Lesson on Gossip from Winston Churchill[45]

We're told this story is true, and believe it to be so. But whether it is fact or make-believe, the point it makes about controlling our speech remains the same.

In the days after World War II, English Prime Minister Winston Churchill was found attending an official ceremony in London. Sitting behind him were two men who recognized the statesman. Shaking their heads in disdain, they began whispering between themselves about the politician in front of them.

"They say Churchill's quite senile now," whispered one.

"Yes, they say he's doing England more harm than good," the other whispered back.

"They say he should step aside and leave the running of this government to younger, more dynamic people," continued the first man.

Then, quite abruptly, their malicious gossip ceased when old Churchill turned around and roared, "They also say he's quite deaf!"

*One of the founding fathers of our country, Ben Franklin, had much to share on the topic of self-control. Listen to a smattering of his wise advice gathered here for you.*

## BEN FRANKLIN ON SELF-CONTROL[46]

- If you would be wealthy, think of saving more than getting.
- If you know how to spend less than you get, you have the philosopher's stone.
- Sell not virtue to purchase wealth, nor liberty to purchase power.
- Spare and have is better than spend and crave.
- He that lieth down with dogs shall rise up with fleas.
- Keep your eyes wide open before marriage, half shut afterwards.
- 'Tis easier to suppress the first desire than to satisfy all that follow it.
- He is a governor that governs his passions, and he is a servant that serves them.
- Eat few suppers and you'll need few medicines.

- Eat to live, live not to eat.
- Life with fools consists in drinking; with the wise man, living's thinking.
- The excellency of hogs is fatness; of men, virtue.
- Little strokes, fell great oaks.
- God gives all things to industry.
- Dost thou love life? Then do not squander time; for that's the stuff life is made of.
- The honest man takes pains, and then enjoys pleasures; the knave takes pleasure, and then suffers pains.
- Work as if you were to live 100 years, pray as if you were to die tomorrow.

❧

## THE WORD ON SELF-CONTROL

"So then, let us not be like others, who are asleep, but let us be alert and self-controlled. For those who sleep, sleep at night, and those who get drunk, get drunk at night. But since we belong to the day, let us be self-controlled, putting on faith and love as a breastplate, and the hope of salvation as a helmet."

—1 Thessalonians 5:6–8

"We all make many mistakes, but those who control their tongues can also control themselves in every other way. We can make a large horse turn around and go wherever we want by means of a small bit in its mouth. And a tiny rudder makes a huge ship turn wherever the pilot wants it to go, even though the winds are strong. So also, the tongue is a small thing, but what enormous damage it can do."

—James 3:2–5 NLT

*"Like a city whose walls are
broken down is a man
who lacks self-control."*
Proverbs 25:28

"All athletes practice strict self-control. They do it to win a prize that will fade away, but we do it for an eternal prize. So I run straight to the goal with purpose in every step. I am not like a boxer who misses his punches. I discipline my body like an athlete, training it to do what it should. Otherwise, I fear that after preaching to others I myself might be disqualified."

—1 Corinthians 9:25–27 NLT

"So prepare your minds for service and have self-control. All your hope should be for the gift of grace that will be yours when Jesus Christ is shown to you."

—1 Peter 1:13 NCV

ᴄ✔

## DISCIPLINE OF THE HEART
by Amy Nappa and Jody Brolsma

On her wedding day, Shari Hayes was a size 20. Her new husband loved her, and friends who had gathered on this special day declared she looked radiant. But Shari felt differently inside.

"I didn't like myself," she shares. "I knew God loved me no matter what, but He wanted to work in my life and make me grow."

So shortly after her wedding day and with the support of her husband, Dan, Shari began one of the ultimate tests of self-control. A diet.

Yes, we've all been on diets. Some with success, most without. Shari had tried other diets too, but this time she was determined to succeed. So instead of starving herself with celery sticks and grapefruit juice, or counting every calorie, Shari made big changes in her life.

First, of course, was eating. "I had to change my eating habits and learn how to eat right." Next, she disciplined herself in exercise. "Exercise can be hard," she admits, "I tried to exercise with a friend for accountability, fun, and encouragement." She sought encouragement from the Scriptures by hanging verses about her home to help her say "no" to temptation. And her loving husband added incentive by offering her a dollar for every pound lost. "We didn't have a lot of money, but a little helped."

Sounds so simple, but we all know from experience that it wasn't. The self-control required for dieting is long-term, not just turning down dessert once a week. Shari remembers, "The hardest part was that it took a long time. One and a half years, slow and steady. It was a long haul but it paid off." Of course Shari got discouraged at times, but instead of indulging in chocolate cake, she treated herself to a new scarf or a video. And the compliments of friends who noticed her slimmer body did wonders to keep her on course as well.

As a result of the discipline of those long months Shari lost eighty pounds. She went from a size 20 to a size 8. Dan gave her the $80 and she went out to spend it all on new, smaller, clothes. And, even more amazingly, Shari has kept that weight off for more than ten years. This truly was a permanent change of lifestyle for her.

Is thinness a virtue? No. However, discipline and self-control are, and Shari certainly has demonstrated these in her life. She doesn't hide away her wedding pictures. Instead, she's proud to tell others of how God helped her reach a difficult goal. She is teaching her daughters a healthful lifestyle and, most importantly, is teaching them to follow God.

Shari encourages us in her own words:

"Seek the Lord when you know God wants you to do something. I wanted to please Him most of all. My motivation was to make the Lord proud and ask for His strength in my weakness. He wants to give us victory through anything that is pleasing to Him. Don't give up. Keep going toward your goal even if you feel it's too far away."

*Loving God, You have the strength to move mountains. Give us the strength to move away from the refrigerator.*

## DIETRICH BONHOEFFER ON TEMPTATION[47]

In our members there is a slumbering inclination towards desire which is both sudden and fierce. With irresistible power, desire seizes mastery over the flesh. All at once a secret, smoldering fire is kindled. The flesh burns and is in flames. It makes no difference whether it is sexual desire or ambition or vanity or desire for revenge or love of fame and power or greed for money or, finally, that strange desire for the beauty of the world, of nature. Joy in God is. . . extinguished in us and we seek all our joy in the creature. At this moment God is quite unreal to us, He loses all reality, and only desire for the creature is real; the only reality is the devil. Satan does not fill us with hatred of God, but with forgetfulness of God. . . . The lust thus aroused envelopes the mind and will of man in deepest darkness. The powers of clear discrimination and of decision are taken from us.

*Adam and Eve's failure to exercise self-control at the dawn of creation had devastating consequences. It's a grim memory, but one by which we can be reminded of the benefits of resisting temptation.*

## BETRAYAL IN THE GARDEN
## (GENESIS 3)

Now the serpent was more crafty than any of the wild animals the LORD God had made. He said to the woman, "Did God really say, 'You must not eat from any tree in the garden'?"

The woman said to the serpent, "We may eat fruit from the trees in the garden, but God did say, 'You must not eat fruit from the tree that is in the middle of the garden, and you must not touch it, or you will die.' "

"You will not surely die," the serpent said to the woman. "For God knows that when you eat of it your eyes will be opened, and you will be like God, knowing good and evil."

When the woman saw that the fruit of the tree was good for food and pleasing to the eye, and also desirable for gaining wisdom, she took some and ate it. She also gave some to her husband, who was with her, and he ate it. Then the eyes of both of them were opened, and they realized they were naked; so they sewed fig leaves together and made coverings for themselves.

Then the man and his wife heard the sound of the LORD God as he was walking in the garden in the cool of the day, and they hid from the LORD God among the trees of the garden. But the LORD God called to the man, "Where are you?"

He answered, "I heard you in the garden, and I was afraid because I was naked; so I hid."

And he said, "Who told you that you were naked? Have you eaten from the tree that I commanded you not to eat from?"

The man said, "The woman you put here with me—she gave me some fruit from the tree, and I ate it."

Then the LORD God said to the woman, "What is this you have done?"

The woman said, "The serpent deceived me, and I ate."

So the LORD God said to the serpent, "Because you have done this,

"Cursed are you above all the livestock
and all the wild animals!
You will crawl on your belly
and you will eat dust

all the days of your life.
And I will put enmity
between you and the woman,
and between your offspring and hers;
he will crush your head,
and you will strike his heel."

To the woman he said,
    "I will greatly increase your pains
in childbearing; with pain you will
give birth to children.
Your desire will be for your husband,
and he will rule over you."

To Adam he said,
    "Because you listened to your wife
and ate from the tree about which I
commanded you, 'You must not eat of it,'
Cursed is the ground because of you;
through painful toil you will eat of it
all the days of your life.
It will produce thorns and thistles for you,
and you will eat the plants of the field.
By the sweat of your brow
you will eat your food
until you return to the ground,
since from it you were taken;

for dust you are
and to dust you will return."

Adam named his wife Eve, because she would become the mother of all the living.

The LORD God made garments of skin for Adam and his wife and clothed them. And the LORD God said, "The man has now become like one of us, knowing good and evil. He must not be allowed to reach out his hand and take also from the tree of life and eat, and live forever." So the LORD God banished him from the Garden of Eden to work the ground from which he had been taken. After he drove the man out, he placed on the east side of the Garden of Eden cherubim and a flaming sword flashing back and forth to guard the way to the tree of life.

# A PRAYER OF SELF-CONTROL FROM WILLIAM BARCLAY[48]

O God,

Control my tongue.

Keep me from saying things which make trouble, and from involving myself in arguments which only make bad situations worse and which get nowhere. Control my thoughts.

Shut the door of my mind against all envious and jealous thoughts; shut it against all bitter and resentful thoughts; shut it against all ugly and unclean thoughts.

Help me live today in purity, in humility, and in love.

Through Jesus Christ my Lord. Amen.

# ABOUT THE AUTHORS

Mike & Amy Nappa are founders of the Christian media organization, Nappaland Communications, Inc. They are best-selling authors with over a half-million copies of their books in print, and have been featured in national TV, radio, and print media. They both serve as contributing editors for *CBA Frontline* magazine, write a weekly column for *CBN Online,* and write monthly columns for *ParentLife* and *Living with Teenagers* magazines. Additionally, their writing has appeared in many other fine publications such as *CCM, Children's Ministry, Christian Parenting Today, Christian Single, FamilyFun, Focus on the Family Clubhouse* and *Clubhouse Jr., Group, Home Life, New Man, Profile, Release,* and more. The Nappas make their home in Colorado where they're active in their church. To contact Mike and Amy, send e-mail to Nappaland@aol.com.

# CREDITS

# Notes

## The Fruit of the Spirit Is. . .
## Love

1. As quoted in *The Christian's Treasury* edited and compiled by Lissa Roche. (Crossway Books, 1995).

2. As told in *Humor for Preaching and Teaching*, edited by Edward K. Rowell. (Baker Book House, 1996).

## The Fruit of the Spirit Is. . .
## Joy

3. As quoted in *Eerdmans' Book of Famous Prayers*, compiled by Veronica Zundel. (Grand Rapids, Mich.: William B. Eerdmans Publishing Company, 1983), 51.

4. *1001 Great Stories and Quotes* by R. Kent Hughes. (Wheaton, Ill.: Tyndale House Publishers, 1998), 304.

5. As quoted in *Ask Me If I Care* by Nancy Rubin. (Berkeley, Calif.: Ten Speed Press, 1994), 147.

6. *Worship and Service Hymnal.* (Chicago, Ill.: Hope Publishing Company, 1957), hymn number 365.

7. Source for language translations is *Travlang's Translating Dictionary*, http://dictionaries.travlang.com/

8. As quoted in *Conversations with God*, edited by James Melvin Washington, Ph.D. (New York: Harper Collins Publishers, 1994), 190.

9. *America in Search of Its Soul* by Gibson Winter. (Harrisburg, Pa.: Morehouse Publishing, 1996), 2–3.

10. As quoted in *Eerdmans' Book of Famous Prayers*, compiled by Veronica Zundel. (Grand Rapids, Mich.: William B. Eerdmans Publishing Company, 1983), 30.

## The Fruit of the Spirit Is. . . Patience

11. As quoted in *The Doubleday Prayer Collection*, selected and arranged by Mary Batchelor. (New York: Doubleday, 1992 & 1996), 412.

12. *It Takes Endurance* by Eugene Robinson. (Sisters, Ore.: Multnomah Publishers, 1998), 16–17.

13. As quoted in *The Communion of Saints*, edited by Horton Davies. (Grand Rapids, Mich.: William B. Eerdmans Publishing Company, 1990), 94.

14. From *Expository Dictionary of Bible Words*, (Grand Rapids, Mich.: Regency Reference Library, 1985), 478.

15. "Why We Pray," *Life* (March 1994): 58.

16. *In the Trenches* by Reggie White. (Nashville, Tenn.: Thomas Nelson Publishers, 1996), 173–85.

## THE FRUIT OF THE SPIRIT IS. . . KINDNESS

17. As quoted by Frederick Buechner in "What are We Going to Be?" *Preaching Today*, Tape 56.

18. As quoted in *The Book of Virtues,* edited, with commentary, by William J. Bennett. (New York: Simon & Schuster, 1993), 147.

19. As quoted in *The Communion of the Saints*, edited by Horton Davies. (Grand Rapids, Mich.: William B. Eerdmans Publishing Company, 1990).

20. "The Big Picture: Staying Afloat" by Charles Hirshberg. *Life* (August 1996): 8.

21. As quoted in *Illustrations Unlimited* (Wheaton, Ill.: Tyndale House Publishers, Inc, 1988), 119.

22. As quoted in *Letters Home* by George Grant and Karen Grant. (Nashville, Tenn.: Cumberland House, 1997), 82–83.

## THE FRUIT OF THE SPIRIT IS. . . GOODNESS

23. From *The Day America Told the Truth,* by James Patterson and Peter Kim. (New York: Prentice Hall Press, 1991), 119–27.

24. "Tiny Archibald, Basketball Hall of Famer" by John O'Keefe. *Sports Illustrated* (November 9, 1998): 22.

25. "Personal Glimpses: Encouraging Words" by Stephen Rubello. *Reader's Digest* (February 1996): 125–26.

26. *The Knowledge of the Holy* by A.W. Tozer. (San Francisco, Calif.: Harper & Row Publishers, 1961).

27. As quoted in *A Treasury of Wisdom*, compiled by Ken and Angela Abraham. (Uhrichsville, Ohio: Barbour Publishing, 1996), July 4 page.

28. Zondervan Publishing House e-mail Alert Service, M|Wire, June 25 and September 17, 1998.

29. Zondervan Publishing House e-mail Alert Service, *The Pastor's File*, April 1998.

30. Zondervan News Service, September 1998.

31. A note to the reader: We originally discovered this story in the encouraging book *And the Angels Were Silent* by Max Lucado.

   However, when we contacted the publisher of that book, they informed us that Max Lucado had obtained the details of the story and the quotes of John Blanchard from an unknown source. If you know, and can verify, the original source, please contact Barbour Publishing so we can properly credit this story in future editions of this book.

32. As quoted in *Letters Home* by George Grant and Karen Grant. (Nashville, Tenn.: Cumberland House, 1997), 165–66.

33. *America's Dumbest Dates*, by Merry Block Jones. (Andrews McMeel Publishing, 1998), 63.

34. "Love Endures as Memory Goes," *The Arizona Republic* (September 29, 1998): D1–D2.

35. "Workin' 5 to 9" by Edward K. Rowell. *Leadership* (April 15, 1998).

36. Phone interview with Max Lucado, conducted by Mike Nappa on September 3, 1998.

37. As quoted in *Thoughts for the Journey 1999 Calendar* (Wheaton, Ill.: Tyndale House Publishers, 1998), January 9, 1999 page.

## THE FRUIT OF THE SPIRIT IS. . .
### GENTLENESS

38. *The Doubleday Prayer Collection*, selected and arranged by Mary Batchelor. (New York: Doubleday, 1992 & 1996), 421.

39. Quoted from *The Lion, the Witch and the Wardrobe* by C. S. Lewis. (New York: Collier Books, 1950), 160–61.

40. As quoted in *The Doubleday Prayer Collection*, selected and arranged by Mary Batchelor. (New York: Doubleday, 1992 & 1996), 421.

## THE FRUIT OF THE SPIRIT IS. . .
### SELF-CONTROL

41. "Doctors fined for brawl during operation." *The Coloradoan* (Sunday, November 28, 1993): A3.

42. *Sinbad's Guide to Life* by Sinbad with David Ritz. (New York: Bantam Books, 1997), 81–82.

43. Statistics taken from: "Closing in on Addiction" by Kristin Leutwyler and Alan Hall. *Scientific American* web site, November 24, 1997; "What If. . ." by various authors. *American Demographics* (December 1997): 39–45; and *The National Clearinghouse for Alcohol and Drug Information* web site.

44. As quoted in *The Book of Virtues*, edited and with commentary by William J. Bennett. (New York: Simon and Schuster, 1993), 48.

45. *Humor for Preaching and Teaching* edited by Ed Rowell. (Grand Rapids, Mich.: Baker Books, 1996), 48.

46. As quoted in *The Moral of the Story* compiled and edited by Jerry Newcombe. (Nashville, Tenn.: Broadman & Holman Publishers, 1996), 145–46, 249, 258–59, 288–89.

47. As quoted in *The Tale of the Tardy Oxcart* by Charles R. Swindoll. (Nashville, Tenn.: Word Publishing, 1998), 566.

48. As quoted in *The Doubleday Prayer Collection*, selected and arranged by Mary Batchelor. (New York: Doubleday, 1992 & 1996), 425.

# Inspirational Library

Beautiful purse/pocket-size editions of Christian classics bound in flexible leatherette. These books make thoughtful gifts for everyone on your list, including yourself!

*When I'm on My Knees*     The highly popular collection of devotional thoughts on prayer, especially for women.
> Flexible Leatherette . . . . . . . . . .$4.97

*The Bible Promise Book*     Over 1,000 promises from God's Word arranged by topic. What does God promise about matters like: Anger, Illness, Jealousy, Love, Money, Old Age, and Mercy? Find out in this book!
> Flexible Leatherette . . . . . . . . . .$3.97

*Daily Wisdom for Women*     A daily devotional for women seeking biblical wisdom to apply to their lives. Scripture taken from the New American Standard Version of the Bible.
> Flexible Leatherette . . . . . . . . . .$4.97

*My Daily Prayer Journal*     Each page is dated and features a Scripture verse and ample room for you to record your thoughts, prayers, and praises. One page for each day of the year.
> Flexible Leatherette . . . . . . . . . .$4.97

Available wherever books are sold.
Or order from:

Barbour Publishing, Inc.
P.O. Box 719
Uhrichsville, OH 44683
http://www.barbourbooks.com